Death by Envy

Dear Leonard —
I found this small tome
among the remains of my
office library (still unpack-
ing since retiring 2 yrs
ago!), and thought it
might be one you would
like for your own reference
collection.

    with love for a dear
friend & colleague,
        Bonnie 11/19/2015
        Peace.

Death by Envy

✦

The Evil Eye and Envy
in the Christian Tradition

Fr. George R. A. Aquaro

iUniverse, Inc.
New York Lincoln Shanghai

Death by Envy
The Evil Eye and Envy in the Christian Tradition

iUniverse, Inc.

For information address:
iUniverse, Inc.
2021 Pine Lake Road, Suite 100
Lincoln, NE 68512
www.iuniverse.com

Based on a thesis submitted to the faculty of St. Vladimir's Orthodox Theological Seminary Master of Divinity Program, Spring 2001.

ISBN: 0-595-30770-1

Printed in the United States of America

Contents

Acknowledgements

God has given me much, and for this I am grateful. He has given me a patient and loving wife, Barbara, who has supported me through thick and thin. He has given me beautiful children, full of life. He has given me caring parents and many friends, both old and new, for which I am not deserving. God remember the brethren in Lompoc!

I would like to thank His Grace, Bishop JOSEPH (al-Zehlaoui) of the Antiochian Orthodox Christian Archdiocese of North America, who convinced me to attend seminary (where this book was conceived) under the blessing and care of His Eminence, Metropolitan PHILIP. Of course, no American Orthodox education experience is complete without V. Rev. Fr. Paul Nadim Tarazi's energetic lectures, and I am grateful to him for getting me to read the Scriptures with his Middle Eastern eye.

I owe much to The Very Reverend Protosyngellos Paul Doyle for his continuous gentle coaching on the art of sanity.

And, this book never would have come to pass were it not for my friend Bill (Vasili) Bassakyros, who convinced me to investigate the Evil Eye. I never imagined it would end up going where it did.

Introduction

e′vil eye′, *n.* **1.** A look thought capable of inflicting injury or bad luck on the person at whom it is directed. **2.** The power, superstitiously attributed to certain persons, of inflicting injury or bad luck by such a look.[1]
fas′cinate, *v.*...**5.** *Obs.* to cast under a spell by a look.[2]
o′verlook *v.*...**9.** *Archaic.* To look upon with the Evil Eye; bewitch.[3]

baskaino 1 aor. **1.** *Bewitch,* as with the Evil Eye, *someone.* **2.** *Envy somebody.*[4]
baskania, -as, -i envy.[5]
baskanias, -ou, -o (both noun and adj.) *the envious one.*[6]

qanah,...**2.** NH *[Late Hebrew].* jealousy; **3.** zeal, envy.[7]
ra ayin,...**9.** One evil of eye.[8]

The Evil Eye is one of the most widespread and beliefs in the world. It has impacted countless people all over the world in every era. It is rooted in envy, something shared by all men in the tragedy of the fallen world. In the modern era, the definition of envy has changed. While most people in our present-day culture do not think much about envy or the Evil Eye, both concepts are still operative under different aliases.

The Evil Eye as a term has been relegated to the Dustbin of Superstition, and now the modern American (by definition the trend-setter in what it is to be the Modern Man) has almost totally lost the concept of envy. When it strikes him or those around him, he is puzzled. When Islamic extremists attack American embassies in Africa (killing very few Americans) or high school students shoot at their classmates, television anchormen contort their faces as if to emphasize the "senselessness" of what makes sense to the rest of the world that has not tried as hard to forget envy.

The word "envy" has lost its fearsome meaning, the Evil Eye no longer being a threat. Helmut Schoeck contends that modern man must forget envy in order to have the conspicuous consumption that fuels our economy.[9] The ancient man saw his success in terms of fertility and fruitfulness, both of his wives and his herds. Later, intellectual ability and skills became the means to success. All of these brought with them a certain amount of envy, since one's neighbors are often not born with the same gifts (i.e., not all are born beautiful and thus cannot attract a 'better' spouse or friends). Since fertility and 'good' often seemed unequally distributed without a possibility of attaining equilibrium on one's own, envy came to manifest itself as a destructive equalizer.

In America, with the most thriving economy thus far in the last century, the loss of our sensitivity to envy has resulted in rampant consumerism and a total disregard for others. Men now live to buy and don't care who sees or how others feel, since the average consumer believes that all men have the ability to succeed in the economy if they make the 'right' choices. So, there is neither shame nor guilt in driving a Mercedes Benz past a starving man (after all, he made the wrong choices resulting in his situation), and the driver may only sense the slightest danger that the onlooker might throw a rock and scratch the paint job. Certainly, he is free from the superstition that the beggar will cast the Evil Eye upon him out of envy. The driver is free to buy and use whatever he wants wherever he wants, which frees him to buy more and more. Yet, he is troubled in some way by the beggar. The driver might not fear being cursed, but he may fear being assaulted. For this reason, he may participate in philanthropy or join a political party that promises to "do more." That way, he can dodge the issue of the beggar's envy by making himself an "innocent victim of random violence" when the rock comes flying. He may excuse the man throwing the rock for being underprivileged, uneducated and "unable to do any better." Nobody wants him to be envious, neither does anyone want Islamic terrorists or high school misfits to feel envy either.

The modern American driver certainly will not say that he has been envied. To admit that such a powerful, destructive emotion is at work would force him to modify his lifestyle. Suddenly, the admiring glance at his shining car deteriorates into the source of threat. Worse yet, the driver might have to come to grips with his own envy of others, an admission of his own impotence to gain more than he has already. His car loses its appeal because there is a better one parked in the driveway down the street. His satisfaction is ruined, and he stays awake at night brooding. Our economy depends upon the discontent man not to destroy his neighbor through violence but rather through market competition.

In studying the Evil Eye, one must delve into areas of ancient myth, history, psychology, anthropology and sociology. The challenge of this work has been to pull together an understanding of envy from as many sources as possible, so that we might better understand all of what the Christian message is confronting. Studying the Evil Eye forces the reader to not only more closely examine the teachings of the Church but also the context in which they were given. Ultimately, the reader is then forced to examine himself and his world. Envy has not stopped merely because Americans refuse to acknowledge its existence.

We will begin by exploring the non-Biblical context of the Evil Eye. This is the only way the reader will be able to see how radical the ancient Hebrew and Christian teachings on envy are when compared to the populations historically around them. Further still, this background information will make many of the utterances of the Holy Fathers much clearer as we see the assumptions of their original audiences. The audiences were predominantly Greek or well versed in Greek culture, so the reader will notice a slant there. Furthermore, Greek philosophers and poets struggled with envy a great deal, leaving us a fantastic amount of literature by which we might better understand this topic.

The final part of this paper will deal with the modern issues surrounding envy and the Evil Eye. The intent here is to provoke further exploration of envy in our personal lives and within our parish communities. Perhaps we can see how defiled we have become simply because we have lost the word "envy" and have forgotten to acknowledge this sin. Further still, we might be able to grasp the madness of the modern world, and the people in it driven by passions they have lost the words to identify.

1

Envy and Limited Good

What is the Evil Eye?

Many people are not familiar with the concept of the Evil Eye. One might have read about or heard references to it, but be unfamiliar with its details. It may be a surprise, but some sociologists claim that nearly 75% of the world's population have some kind of belief in the Evil Eye.[10] Though others may argue against this figure, all agree that the belief in the Evil Eye is both wide-spread and ancient.

So, what exactly is the Evil Eye? Essentially, the Evil Eye is a belief that a person's eye produces harmful emanations when he or she feels envy towards another. These emanations often cause harm either to the object that the envious person desires or to the person possessing the object. This harm can range from minor illness to death or destruction, depending on the belief of the community. Sometimes emanations can be involuntary, much as a sudden emotional onset might be possible to gain control of once it has occurred but is hard to prevent at the onset. Some people, because of their character or condition in life, are considered more disposed to casting the Evil Eye even if they desire not to.

A secondary belief regarding the Evil Eye is that it is a magical act of a witch. Witches have the natural ability to cause harm through special inborn gifts, or they can cause harm through sorcery. In sorcery, either a witch or an average person can use an incantation or magical object to put the Evil Eye on another. The underlying motivation is always envy.

It may be helpful at this point to discuss envy as a concept. Envy is defined by *Webster's Unabridged Dictionary* as, "a feeling of discontent or covetousness with regard to another's advantages, success, possessions, etc."[11] A good beginning, but not enough to satisfy most experts. Envy is not merely "a feeling of discontent" but a desire to do harm to another person perceived by the envious as having an advantage. The noted Sociologist Helmut Schoeck identifies envy as the single most powerful emotion a human is capable of experiencing.[12] Why? A

1

summary of Schoeck's findings identifies a number of factors that add up to a shockingly desperate situation for the envious:

- A survey of all literature on envy reveals the universal presence of both high anxiety and destructive behavior in relation to the emotion.

- Envy results in the isolation of the envious from his fellow men.

- At the same time, envy is bound up with feelings of inadequacy driving him to compare himself to others, and thus the envious cannot escape the source of his pain.

- Envy is an admission of inadequacy, and therefore is almost never honestly confessed.

- There are no reciprocal feelings involved with envy (i.e., the envious do not want those they envy to return the same emotion).

- Even if the envious sees the envied destroyed, the root of inadequacy within himself remains unchanged (i.e., there is no easing of pain once the envied one is deprived of his advantage).

- Envy cannot easily be artistically depicted, nor can it be institutionalized in a positive sense (e.g., we can have national holidays to grieve the dead, but we cannot have a holiday devoted to envy).

- There is no way to mollify envy other than completion of the act of destruction (e.g., lust for another may be eased through masturbation, but there is almost no "Plan B" for dealing with envy).

- Envy has no positive attributes (e.g., unlike anger or guilt)[13]

Envy is so powerful that Schoeck theorizes that it is the need that drives human beings to form societies and cultures,[14] giving men protection from one another's envy by establishing a status quo. Psychologists and sociologists agree that envy is universal,[15] and as evidence we present that the oldest body of written literature, that of the Sumerians, is preserved almost exclusively as business contracts. Thousands upon thousands of clay business contracts. All to protect ancient Sumerians from the envious behavior of fellow citizens (i.e., the violation of business agreements). Envy is powerful enough to influence a great deal of human behavior and complex enough to defy resolution. No society has ever eliminated envy.

In the field of psychology, the roots of envy are unclear. There appears to be no agreement on whether the capacity to envy is present at birth or if it is a later derivative of more primitive urges as a child develops.[16] It would seem that envy necessitates a strong sense of self and awareness of others as separate identities, neither of which are traits of a newborn. Envy would appear to be an option once a child can discern and choose between himself and another. Once the envious assault has begun, it sets the stage for what can be a downward spiral of attack and counter-attack, played out in vindictiveness and prophylactic violence.[17]

Jealousy is often erroneously used interchangeably with envy. While envy is the desire for something that one does not possess, jealousy has to do with the protection of what one already has from another who is in a position to take the possession away.[18] This means there is a rival, usually a peer, but this can be stretched to include superiors, inferiors and even objects. The relationship between the jealous and his possession is that the jealous person derives identity from the possession (often seen as irreplaceable by the possessor) and so its loss not only involves being deprived of the object but also deprived of part of one's identity. Therefore, to be jealous of an object is also to guard one's self-definition against assault. Richard Coss points out that with jealousy there sometimes appears to be a need to be needed which triggers this emotion.[19]

We should add that jealousy implies a limited quantity, something we will discuss later. In fact, we can say that jealousy can only be understood in terms of singularity. To be jealous of something is to see it as single and irreplaceable, so that its loss means there cannot be a replacement. This will become clearer later when we discuss God's jealousy for Israel, or the virtue of being jealous "for God." Thus, jealousy can have a positive side.

History of Evil Eye Beliefs

Other terms we should be familiar with are covetousness and greed. In the minds of Classical Greeks, these terms served as the sources of envy. It is this passion to possess that initiates envious behavior. What must be noted is that Greeks did not go beyond blaming "the material" for the passions, the error made by Karl Marx and later socialists when they proposed the redistribution of wealth. Greeks saw both material (i.e., possessions, land, etc.) and non-material (i.e. intelligence, beauty, etc.) as sources for envy. While the Greeks differentiated envy from covetousness (inordinate desire for wealth or possessions, a synonym for greed),[20] the philosophers had very little agreement as to what caused either passion.

What we must recognize is that the envious man uses the possessions of others as the contact point of to human relationships.[21] People are no longer valued for who they are but rather by what they have, and what they have effects how they are treated. The other person simply becomes the sum total of their possessions when envy "infects the eyes" as St. Basil the Great wrote in his homily *On Envy*.[22]

Belief in the Evil Eye goes back to ancient Sumeria, to some 5,000 years before Christ.[23] Amidst the many thousands of ancient clay tablets are several prayers for the Evil Eye and home remedies. Although there are no long theological discourses on the nature of the Evil Eye, it is clear from the remaining prayers that it causes nuisances such as broken farm equipment and loss of fertility.[24]

This belief spread over time to the later Babylonians and all the peoples of the "Fertile Crescent" of Mesopotamia. Again, we have no records from that period and historical information is limited at best. What we do know is that by the time of writing of the Old Testament books, the Evil Eye is a well-developed belief and ingrained in the cultures of the Near East.

Philosophers of ancient Greece not only believed in the power of the Evil Eye, but also developed natural sciences to explain in a rational manner how the eye can communicate such power. The ancient Greeks (and possibly those before them) believed that the eye produced light, which Plato theorized combined with daylight to produce a link between the soul and the world.[25] Various theories tried to account for how the image returned to the eye, but to no substantive agreement.

Some believed that vision was communicated through impressions made in the air, which passed through the pupil into the eye,[26] while Leucippus and Democritus believed that atoms forming emanations or images (*eidola*) from the object combined with *eidola* from the viewer's eye and return to it.[27] A consensus could not be reached, and philosophers such as Plato confined their observations to emanations rather than the mechanics of reception. The Greeks thought of light as a material affair. Whether light is its own matter or an impression on matter, being in contact with light meant being in contact with the object giving off light.

With Euclid's book *Optics*, the Greeks learned that light traveled in rays, conforming to Pythagoras' theories of geometry. This book became the authority on the mechanics of vision until the 11th century Arab philosopher Alhazen revolutionized the study of light by his studies of the *camera obscura* (or "darkened chamber") which theorized that light was not a form of matter.[28] Alhazen saw light as an active force, and that he understood it was not necessary for the eye to produce light to draw in the world. It was not until the European Renaissance that Alhazen's conclusions were applied to the burgeoning study of anatomy, and Leonardo da Vinci suggested that the eye was a *camera obscura*, utterly passive to the light of the world.[29] With that, eye emanations and visual rays were relegated to the compost heap of primitive thought.

In brief, we can say that the most ancient beliefs make vision an active process, and that only in a modern context did passive vision theories come to dominate. We are left with the question as to what evidence early man used to reinforce the notion of active vision prior to the Greek philosophers. This is rather simple, since the philosophers actually cite a great deal of natural evidence to support their theories.

The greatest source of evidence for vision as an active process is the very natural aversion men and animals have to being stared at. The Greeks theorized that animals had power in their eyes, which they either directly used or employed through characteristic "eye spots" to generate a hypnotic effect. Animals such as wolves (who often gaze with a fixed stare) and peacocks (for their many spotted feathers) were considered to have an Evil Eye, which they used either in a predatory or defensive manner. The basilisk, a fantastic serpent, was thought to hunt exclusively with an Evil Eye, which has intriguing implications when one considers its employment in Scripture.

Of course, we now know that being looked at is an inborn fear, arising from a natural instinct that to be looked at is the first stage to predatory attack. Eye spots on animals arose to stun predators by creating this instinctual fear by presenting a larger set of eyes, thus the illusion of an even greater animal to face the predator.[30] The momentary hesitation it produces gives the prey a moment to escape. The ancients assumed the "creepy feeling" associated with being looked at had something to do with the power of the eye, making it an entirely external effect. This makes vision something of a magical process. It is mysterious and powerful, much as the forces of nature appear to be in ancient man.

Dualism and Limited Good

Central to any *mythos* is an account as to why both good and bad things happen to men. The world appears capricious and unjust while men crave predictability and order. Social structures arise to protect men from one another and form a communal system to face the constant challenges of nature (or outsiders). The mystery of nature can only be countered by an equally mysterious and powerful social structure, and so the story of the society becomes as mystical as the forces of nature it confronts. Morality is subjective: good and evil are simply defined as things aiding survival versus things threatening extinction.

The forces of good (survival) and evil (extinction) appear to men to be struggling poles in a battle for survival, just as men battle the elements. This is the root of "dualism," a form of primitive thought that locks equal forces of good and evil in a constant war. Soon, the whole world is divided between these two camps: hot and cold, wet and dry, earth and sky, etc. Men do not see those things that manifest power over their lives as neutral.

The noted sociologist George Foster, in his studies of Central American Indians, developed a concept called "Limited Good." This concept, which has been received as a universal principle for understanding peasant thought (both in terms of the historical 'peasant' and the modern person living in a less developed, agrarian culture), applied dualism to daily life and thus organized peasant thought into a rational system. Foster believed that peasants see good and evil as equals pitted in a struggle, but also that good and evil are in limited quantities. This means that there is only so much good to go around, and if you don't have good then you are stuck with evil. Your neighbor's increase of good then deprives you of good and brings you evil. Therefore, peasant societies seek to "level the playing field" by preventing any one person from excelling beyond the average.

This makes sense to the casual observer, especially when looking at the Near East where natural resources are sparse. A single person's overuse of the well means the village water supply will soon be used up. Therefore, the village takes measures of social pressure on anyone whose water activities outstrips their neighbor's consumption levels. The same can be said of grazing land: one shepherd's overabundance can lead to his neighbor's starvation by defoliating the countryside, not to mention driving down prices for meat and wool.

Since peasants usually live in remote regions where outside trade is both difficult and rare, Foster noted that they form closed communities. People rely on one another, thus a balance is necessary. A potter who makes too many pots cannot sell his excess to traders who aren't there, and so his glut drives down prices and causes other potters to lose profits. This can impact the whole community rather quickly, and so people urge one another not to over-produce. Ambition is a negative attribute.

Wet and Dry, Life and Death

Land itself is almost always seen as a limited good. This should be obvious, since it is a non-increasing resource. Land does not expand, and it is almost always divided up by long-held claims. Loss of control over land permanently impoverishes the loser, who no longer has the basic necessities to create wealth (i.e., natural resources) once the land is lost.

This idea of limited good within a community makes for tense social relations. Envy becomes a primary emotion, since the increase of another's good comes at one's own expense. We often see in peasant culture much more of a communal attitude than we find today in terms of sharing. This has a great deal to do with keeping the communal balance: those who share their 'good' with others cannot be accused to taking 'good' from their neighbors. This redistribution of wealth prevents envy in neighbors and reduces the chance of accusations against the "lucky" fellow.

When we think of the Near East and Eastern Mediterranean in terms of climate, we notice that it is primarily an arid region where potable water is limited. The hot summers dry the land and clay soil does not store water, so the seasonal regularity of rain is necessary for survival. Those societies established along waterways also relied on the rivers to follow some type of predictable behavior, so that irrigation could be planned for crops and that the water remained potable.

A season without rain could translate into famine for herdsmen and farmers. Every society was dependent upon regular seasons that guaranteed that water would come neither in an unwieldy flood nor in too light of a rainfall to support life. Water is life, and dryness became associated with death.

We are further reminded of this theme when we think of the ancient Near East theme of chaotic waters in the *mythos* of Marduk and Tiamat. Sumerians and their descendents saw life coming out of water (which could also destroy if not properly restrained.) Life was water, since the world was formed in it. One can get the picture using clay: too little water meant hard dirt, too much water meant mud. The proper amount of water and dirt produced clay, necessary for bricks and pottery, the things of life. The clay was the preexisting matter of the universe, into which the water of life was introduced.

Folklorist Alan Dundes' analysis of Evil Eye beliefs linked to symbolism of Wet and Dry will help us understand how Semitic and Hellenistic peoples understood the world around them,[31] particularly in terms of the Evil Eye. The interplay between the Greeks and Mesopotamia is well and helpful in connecting Greek beliefs to Mesopotamia.[32]

Drawing from Onians' work,[33] Dundes concluded that the Evil Eye, being an evil force, was interpreted by primitive people as a form of drying. The 'limited good' of Foster can be applied to human fluids;[34] thus humans have a finite supply of liquids. The Evil Eye depletes a human of necessary life liquids, and so amulets were made to represent life liquids and thus counteract the effect of the drying threat or deter it.[35] Semen, milk, blood and even spittle are all life fluids by this standard, and symbols of such are enough to drive away dry forces. In the case of the latter, spitting on the devil as performed in the Church may have its source both in it derisive significance as well as its symbolism of man's God-given gift of life overcoming the dry fallen spirits. Baptism can be seen in much the same terms, since water is both life (in reasonable quantity) and death (such as deluge and drowning).

Returning to Greek thought, wet and dry were seen as opposites tied to hot and cold, which comprised the four primary elements.[36] This belief can be traced as far back as Anaximander in the 7th century BC. Throughout later ages, Greek philosophers sought to explain the universe in terms of Wet and Dry, giving various explanations of cosmology invariably linked with principles of fluids and heat. Onians sketched out Greek beliefs in the balance of fluids (e.g., drunkenness as a manifestation of excess fluids rather than a function of toxicity),[37] and in fact the human being as having various necessary fluids in various locations throughout the body. These fluids were in limited supply, and their expenditure meant the end of life.[38] Replenishing was only possible to a limited degree, and as Dundes concluded, the wrinkles on an old man had a strong parallel to those of a raisin, both meeting the same fate.[39]

This accounts both for the Hellenistic practices of embalming and cremation, both of which were designed to hasten the drying process and thus "liberate" the soul from the body sooner rather than later.[40] We can easily discern why the Church opposes cremation not only as disrespectful of the body (i.e. against Platonic thought), but also against dualism (i.e. life and death as Wet and Dry).[41] Further, the prohibitions on embalming are not only in reference to the Biblical concept of man's body returning to the dust from which he was formed, but also to the ancient practice of embalming as desiccation,[42] which is a finalization of the death process through drying.

What we ought to note from this concept of wet and dry is the importance of fluids in the battle against death. It is argued that the only acceptable way (at least in the Greek/Semitic mind) to fight death is by countering it with blood/life fluid, namely a live sacrifice. The shedding of blood to avert a drying force can be seen in the sacrifice of children and animals. Infant sacrifice is evidently a Biblical theme according to Levenson's analysis.[43] In short, Semitic and Greek peoples commonly believed that children were not necessarily their property, but were "owned" to some degree by the gods. Often, the firstborn child was sacrificed by its parents in many cultures of the Mediterranean, especially Carthage and North Africa.[44] A replacement sacrifice of a lamb could be made in its place, but if the child became sick it was assumed the gods were trying to obtain the child.[45] A further shedding of blood (i.e., life liquid) would be necessary to appease the deity. The parents would then only be concerned with fighting off "dry" or evil spirits once the gods were satisfied. This theme dominates the manufacturing of talismans, which come to be symbols of life-giving water (i.e., blue beads [water], red beads [blood], horns [phallus], horseshoes [kteis/female sexual organ], and eyes [both as a warning to the viewer and a symbol of water]).

Luck and Fertility

Returning to the topic of luck, there will be times when a peasant "accidentally" receives an increase of good (i.e., a field becomes extremely productive or animals produce more milk than expected). Men, already keen to unseen forces of nature, believe that there is an invisible power that distributes blessings and curses. This force is called "luck" or *mana* in sociological circles.[46]

All societies have some belief in mana, and it is only in the particulars that the explanations for it vary. Another way of looking at mana is to understand it in terms of honor. A man of honor in a community has special giftings, whether it is a noble birth or special talents that the community depends upon. He has special powers in the eyes of his neighbors, and thus it is only fair that he should be able to own more than others without upsetting the balance of good within the community.

If this man were to suffer "bad luck," people would begin to doubt the merit of his honor and resent his ownership of many possessions. The honor once given to him by the community would be taken away, and he would then be seen as someone who is depriving the community of its good. Honor is the ability to receive luck without resentment. While the average man may receive luck in small quantities, a great deal of luck would cause the community to have to change its view of the neighbor: is he "lucky" and thus more honorable, or is he manipulating the forces of nature to steal from others?

There are others, suffering from the random misfortunes of life, who are considered "unlucky." The random force of luck has struck them (without necessarily a reasonable explanation), and their degraded position means they are deprived of honor. A widow or childless woman is an example of this. She is expected to be destitute, somehow cursed with bad mana.[47]

Magic and Retribution (Honor versus Magic)

One of the greatest sources for concern with luck is its effect on fertility. Fertility is usually seen as a matter of luck. This makes fertility something added to animals (or businesses) which makes them able to produce in abundance, while bad luck means that a barrier has been placed over the animal or activity that makes it unable to produce. The most ancient cultic activity of men centered on fertility, and it was a constant concern because fertility guaranteed survival.

Men have always sought to influence luck. Obviously, the stakes are high: a bout of bad luck could have permanent consequences. Since the average man receives small cases of good and bad luck, he can easily explain his fortunes not in terms of his own efforts (or mistakes) but in the fickle forces of nature. With the balance of the community in question, it is much safer for a peasant to claim luck as the source of his abundant crop of vegetables than his own efforts, since continued efforts would necessarily deprive his neighbors of their share of the good.

It would be natural for a man to hope to prevent bad luck and attract good luck. Now we have the beginnings of magical thought. In this realm, certain objects or charms attract the forces of good mana or repel the evil. Charms go back as far as we have archeological evidence of man. The shape of the object, its symbolic representation, demands that it have a similar power to the original object it is designed to resemble.

The charm can also serve as a reminder. It can be a warning to evil against trying to attack the person wearing the amulet, just like animals employ eye spots to ward off predators. So, amulets can have a natural psychological and a supernatural function.

But, let us go beyond small incidents of luck and assume the extreme. On the one hand, we have those with a great deal of honor. On the other hand, we have those without any honor: the lame, the widowed, the infertile. Those in this latter category have no honor, so they are without possessions and powerless in the eyes of the community.

In dualism, the struggle between good and evil necessitates that evil has its own power. The honorable have the power of good mana or fortune, giving them the right to use force to protect their belongings and their dignity. But those with bad luck have no such resources. Those who could use force would reverse their bad fortune by taking another's property. The truly unfortunate have no such ability, and we can even say that what possessions they have are under the constant threat of seizure because of the weak state of the possessor (i.e., a vulnerable position).

The power of evil is in magic. While those with honor have terrestrial powers to defend themselves and their property, their balancing force on the evil side is magic. This is why old women and the lame were considered to be witches and warlocks: they had the right to practice magic due to their bad luck. This is why they were generally persecuted in a sporadic manner, since it was their right in a dualistic world to exercise the "black arts." Magic is for those who have no honor, and honor must be balanced out.

There are other ways that Foster says balance is brought to a community. Aside from seizure (which requires force and thus a greater level of honor, such as a mob), there is gossiping and accusation. Both keep the honor of peasants in check and the community stabilized. Any one member who begins to excel in the community will quickly find himself the subject of gossip and, if this does not work, accused of using magic for personal gain.

The accusation is tell-tale of envy. It is a hybrid of gossip, yet whereas gossip is general negative talk about a person, an accusation is specific. It is an indictment of a crime. In the case of the honorable, the worst offense one can face is that of being dishonorable and unworthy of what one has. If the charge is accepted, the community will expect the person to give up ownership of all things his new status no longer permits him to own. The accusation is designed to lower honor.

And, at the same time, the accusation very often mirrors the crimes of the community as a whole. The community feels inferior, and thus transfers its inferiority to the honorable. Of course, the community will cull out of its own dishonorable behavior the crimes that it can use in its accusations to bring the honorable down to the community's standard. The envy of the community, which sees the honor it cannot attain to, unleashes slander and accusation to destroy the honorable. By eliminating the honorable, the status quo returns and life goes on as before.

The only exception to this, according to Foster, is when the honor comes from outside the community. Since the community's resources have not been used, it does not feel as though its limited good has been depleted. A successful merchant from a distant land would not trigger the envy of the peasant unless he dares to settle into the peasant's community. Once there, he could become a target because he partakes of the community's limited good.

What this ends up doing is creating a peasant society that emphasizes radical individualism rather than communalism.[48] The leadership positions necessary to enact political communism or anything more complicated that a chief-and-elder system is virtually impossible within such a vindictive community. The shaman is perhaps the lone exception, yet his powers are exclusively magic rather than 'secular' power.

The Greeks and Envy

There have been several authors who have devoted considerable effort to the concept of envy in Greek thought. Our interest in Greek terminology for envy has as much to do with the Hellenistic influences on later Hebrew thought as it preserves some reflections of Semitic thought. Ancient Greek culture arose in the Eastern Mediterranean in close proximity to the various Near Eastern civilizations that anteceded the Sumerians. Of course, the entire New Testament story played out in a Hellenized Near Eastern context, so the exploration of Greek thought will not be without its benefits.

The first term we need to explore is *zelos*. *Zelos* has two primary translations according to Bauer: zeal or ardor, and envy or jealousy.[49] The former is expressed in terms of a positive attribute, while the latter is distinctively negative. Lysias (5th century BC) used this word to express a desire to imitate or emulate, and Philip of Macedonia is counseled by Isocrates that if he unites the Greeks against the Persians he will be *zelotos* or 'admired.'[50] Classicist Peter Walcot found that when zeloswas used opposite *phthonos*, its positive definition is used,[51] as exemplified by Aristotle's second book of Rhetoric. Here, Aristotle found *zelos* to be virtue that can motivate a man to improve himself by emulating a superior.[52]

Hesiod, from the 8th century BC, counseled a lazy brother to work hard and so to become an object of his neighbor's *zelosei* or 'jealousy' as a reward. Here it may better be translated as 'esteem.' In his *Theogony*, Hesiod makes *Zelos* into a God, who is allied with Zeus in his war against the Titans.[53] Isocrates used a verb form of *zelos* when calling a young man to *zeloun* or 'emulate' the manner of kings, and thus gain royal favor.[54] We can say *zelos* is, in this line of thinking, more or less ego-related: it is what one senses others feelings to be of him when one's pride swells.

The same author, in his *Work and Days*, then goes on to present the 'spirit of *zelos*' as "with grim face and screaming voice, who delights in evil."[55] This poem goes further to show Decency and Respect fleeing, signs that ego is at work here as well. The fact that the subject of *zelos* is often brought up in close proximity to discussions of *timé* or 'honor'[56] reinforces this ego relationship.

But what is it that stirs up *zelos*? The answer is, according to Aristotle, "success."[57] Any type of advancement beyond the average is grounds for envy. Obviously, this is linked to the idea of the "limited good" and material well-being or sufficiency, but also in terms of *timé*. This honor can be awarded in several ways in Greek culture: by birth or by ascription of the community.[58] While the former is considered an accident of birth (being born into a noble or royal family is hardly something one can do anything about), it is the latter which accounts for much of the day-to-day envies of the average man.

Philotimia, or 'love of honor,' can be seen as an answer to *zelos* in a negative respect, and can be translated in certain contexts as 'jealousy.'[59] Plutarch wrote that *philotimia* in turn produces envy,[60] since honor itself is relative to one's peers. Someone with *philotimia* will seek to prevent his neighbor from rising in others' esteem (likely motivated by *zelos*), which would thus diminish his own honor in their eyes.[61] Whereas *zelos* is an inferior-to-superior relationship, *philotimia* goes in the opposite direction by envying the good fortune of others of equal or lesser rank. This becomes an important concept when dealing with Greek mythology, where the gods frequently punish men for usurping the glory reserved for deities, while the gods struggle amongst themselves for places of primacy.

But, the risk of being envied was preferable, in common thinking, to being unenviable. Herodotus stepped down from high classical thought when describing how a Corinthian tyrant counseled his son that it is better to be envied than pitied, and Plutarch pointed out that no one envies those struck with misfortune.[62] In the 5th century BC, the poet Pindar acclaimed virtue as giving a dead man "the much envied (*polyzelotos*) crown of glory" as reward for his hard struggles.[63] There are even those Greeks who went as far as to give their children the name *Polyzalos* or "much envied."[64]

Up to this point, *zelos* is confined to those who can reasonably expect to raise themselves to the level of those being emulated. When there is *zelos* downward, it is defined as *hybris*.[65] The definition of *hybris* is insolence, arrogance, shame, insult and mistreatment of an inferior by a superior (it may also be used in terms of natural disasters).[66] In the case of gods and men of high rank, *hybris* is a fully acceptable and socially sanctioned means of preserving rank and social order.[67] Those in power, since they hold responsibility for the social order, were expected by the Greeks to violently preserve their rank or honor from usurpation. To some extent, this must have been a comfort, since Greek mythology had plenty of examples of envy getting out of hand. To know that envy had limits enforced with violence probably helped many Greeks sleep much better.

Phthonos is the next term we need to explore. Unlike *zelos*, this word is employed purely in a negative way to mean 'jealousy' or 'envy.'[68] Aristotle drew a line between the two when he stated that the emulation impulse of *zelos* drives the person experiencing it to go get what his neighbor has, while the person expe-riencing *phthonos* seeks to deprive his neighbor of that very thing.[69] So, *phthonos* takes on not just a desire for a neighbor's possessions, but a confiscatory element: it tries not just to deprive the neighbor of that which is envied, but *phthonos* can drive a god or man to even destroy the object of his envy.[70]

Closer to the reality of daily life, Xenophon described *phthonos* simply as annoyance with one's friends' successes.[71] Having seen the destructive side of *phthonos* in Greek mythology, Isocrates warned that those who excel must work daily at being kind to others lest they face *phthonos*.[72] It is Plutarch who turns to a very Christian approach (sometime before Christ!): he exhorted men to be gen-erous towards enemies, since it roots out habits of hatred and jealousy which eventually are aimed at friends.[73] Hesiod, on the other hand, believed that envy is simply part of human life, and so it is best directed at enemies so that we have none left for friends, while Themistocles advised men to harness *phthonos* until it becomes *zelos*.[74] The modern Turk continues the ancient Greek practice of giving the bearer of good news a tip or "sop," thus assuaging his messenger's *phthonos* by sharing his gift (an example of this can be seen in Sophocles' *Trachiniae*).[75]

Greeks feared the degeneration of *zelos* into *phthonos*, and went to lengths to avoid envy. Amongst the 5th century Athenians, one had to watch not only the malevolent actions of envious friends and enemies, but the very real threat of ostracism by the democratic community.[76] Philanthropy had much less to do with the root word ('love of man') as it had with securing not only *timé* but also avoiding other people's *phthonos* of one's success.[77] Walcot argues that Athenian democracy served to help relieve an envy-torn culture by leveling men somewhat by establishing a universal peerage with ostracism as its enforcement (though he questions whether this was intentional).[78]

We must address this issue of peers as the target of *phthonos*. *Zelos* may be experienced among peers or towards the upper class, but it does not appear that *phthonos* nor *zelos* is experienced towards an inferior (unless we are speaking of preserving honor through *hybris*). In the case of peasant society, there are no infe-riors to look down upon since all are equally dependent on the 'limited good' that Foster describes. The upper classes may be resented in some way, but not with the venom with which a peasant feels envy towards a neighbor.

We must, at this point, return to the subject of dualism brought up earlier in this endeavor. Dualism's end result is the surrender of man to omnipresent evil (at least in this life). Such a worldview makes *phthonos* an unavoidable part of human life. As mentioned earlier, Greek thought made no effort to separate *phthonos* from man's ontology. Rather, envy was explored in terms of its work in the conscious and subconscious, and literature simply warned of this evil residing in the heart on a permanent basis.

Having now passed through the preliminary jargon, we shall now look at Hellenistic patterns of how one reacts to feelings of envy. In examining *zelos*, we noticed that emulation and positive motivation to improve one's self can result from moderate levels of *zelos*. As one's *zelos* increases, the power of the desire demands quicker appeasement as it transforms into *phthonos*. Also, the focus of desire becomes less generalized (i.e., having something similar) and more specific (i.e., having *that* one). The resulting action would be seizure of what is desired. Theft, clearly motivated by this passionate desire, is too great a topic to explore within this paper so we shall pass by it without further comment, other than to say that Evil Eye has little to do with this.[79] We are more concerned with the alternative for those unable to steal or to possess (because they do not have sufficient mana or luck): the destruction of the envied. This destructive envy is called *vaskanía*.

Vaskanía means both envy and Evil Eye, both in verb and noun forms. The other terms we have explored describe a motivation for actions, a root cause as it were. *Vaskanía* describes an action as an emotional state.

As we have seen from the previous vocabulary examples, the Greeks understood that jealousy and envy necessitated certain actions. I think it is safe to say that the Greeks would not have understood envy as a concept without a resulting activity (i.e., one cannot have an emotion which does not effect one's actions). But, *vaskanía's* real emotional power as a word comes from its verb root, *baskaino* (the letter 'v' in *vaskanía* in is the modern Greek pronunciation, represented by the letter beta). The envy itself is the action; in the envying, the assault has also taken place.

The action has been made, the "touch" of the glance has left its soiled print. *Vaskanía* implies instant victimization, as the word used for those struck by *vaskanía* is *baskanothenai*, which is often translated as 'maligned.'[80] A curious observation is that the author of this paper was unable to find a future tense for the word, nor is there an instance when one prepared himself to act this way. *Vaskanía* seems to have an inherent suddenness that might explain the common understanding that one can unintentionally cast the eye. The impulse of a momentary passion is all that it takes.

Zelos and *phthonos* have been described by the poets in terms of kings and gods. What also divorces *vaskanía* from the other terms is the social setting in which it occurs, namely amongst common people and peasants. The lexicographer Hesychius describes the one exception in mythical craftsmen known as

Telchines, who are envious (in the professional sense towards one another), but also magicians and *baskanoi*.[81] Of course, craftsmen were always peasants, so even here we have mythical peasants. Greek writers, such as Strabo and Diodoros Siculus, used the Telchines to describe the common problem of professional envy found amongst Greek craftsmen and shopkeepers. However, this type of envy was linked to them also being magicians, more than just average peasant activity. Or, is it? *Vaskanía* here means something more malignant than *phthonos*, yet it is assumed to be widespread, laying just under the veneer of daily peasant activity.

Plutarch's *Moralia* states that common men do not fear envy, just as the poor do not fear sycophants.[82] In his mind, equality or commonality of peasant life washes away the possibility of such deep emotions as *zelos* and *phthonos*, but he leaves *vaskanía* unmentioned. This is easy to see, given the subject matter and the social circle with which Greek philosophers and writers concerned themselves. They explored human conditions using gods and heroes, where the extremes of *zelos* and *phthonos* played out in the drama of mythology. Certainly the gods had human traits, but there was more than a touch of romanticism and fantasy in their characterization. The average Athenian shopkeeper may have had a temper, but could it be as bad as Zeus'? Shopkeepers do not throw lightning bolts at one another, nor do they unleash phalanxes of warriors against competitors. What do they have left to strike with?

Baskaino as a verb is often synthetically separated into 'envy' or 'witchcraft' during the translation process. While many uses that appear in Greek texts could be adequately translated as 'jealous' or 'envious' without mentioning 'witchcraft,' it is not sufficient to say that these words in English translate the entire meaning of the word as a Greek would read it. More often than not, *vaskanía* is meant to express a type of witchcraft or dark force (or mana) associated with the experience of envy. Sometimes translated mistakenly as 'bewitched,' *vaskanía* cannot be mistaken only for the hypnotic sense this word is often used with in modern times.

An example of the hypnotic meaning can be seen when Theocritus tells of a Cyclops who, finding his reflection it the ocean to be quite beautiful, spat upon his own chest three times to ensure he had not 'bewitched' (*baskantho*) himself.[83] The clearest example of this was the mythological Narcissus, who so fell in love with his own image in a pool that he forsook all food and drink to the point of death in favor of gazing at himself.[84] Narcissus is an important teaching tool for Greek thought on this subject: 1) the wasting associated with envy, 2) the danger of praising or esteeming something too highly, 3) the self-centeredness inherent in envy, 4) that one's feelings of longing are illusory and 5) the ultimate destruction of the thing envied, in this case, the image in the pool.

Clearly, the Greeks saw that to have envy or deep longing for something was not pleasant. Insatiable cravings are the admission that one is incomplete, to have such cravings for something one cannot have is tragic. That Narcissus wasted away while desiring his own beauty shows the ultimate futility and destructive nature of envy in the deepest reaches of Greek thought: humans have within themselves all they truly need, and longing for something outside the self is to long for something already possessed. But, Narcissus' death raises another problem: is the wasting death simply the final revelation of Narcissus' inner state? Was Narcissus inwardly a dead bag of bones, and his self-hypnosis merely a means by which the outside world came to know of his empty condition?

Self-destruction seems to be the ultimate lot for those who are envious. This accounts for Cicero and countless others who warn men not to look too closely at something. To stir up desire for something can bring ruin if such a thing stays out of one's grasp. *Vaskanía* takes on its most malicious definition when the sufferer realizes that the subject envied is beyond his grasp. This makes *vaskanía* a problem of the shopkeeper and pauper, not the gods. Zeus could be *jealous* of a mortal's achievement because it detracts from his divine honor, and he might have be stirred to destroy a man. But, Zeus was also quite capable of doing whatever men do with little effort. For him, *vaskanía* was not an issue, because he was capable of taking what he wants. The pauper who does not have and cannot have, he is more likely to suffer from and act out with *vaskanía*.

Siebers argued that Narcissus' tale pointedly shows that he was not 'narcissistic' in the sense that we use the term, but rather that Narcissus became focal point of his community's envy.[85] The Boeotian community envied Narcissus and cursed him, thus making Narcissus' narcissism a projection of their collective envy. Narcissism is, in this case, the accusation rather than the condition of the accused. The Boeotians confessed their envy and narcissism in their accusation of Narcissus. This is a classic case of what psychologists call 'transference.'[86]

Beyond this, Siebers also pointed out that the accusation against Narcissus is a bit over the top.[87] His apparent self-love had no ill effects on the Boeotians other than the fact that he was separated from his community by not having need of any of them. This lack of need was reinterpreted as a supernatural power, worse yet an appearance that his possession of good (manifested by his lack of need for them) was at the Boeotians' expense. Narcissus was given special powers by the community to be a threat *to the community*. The powers did not actually exist, but there was and is power in the accusation.

This curse was a desperate act, totally devoid of hope or acceptance. The act of *vaskanía*, whether intentional or otherwise, unveils the envious suffering to the degree where love and respect are totally defeated. The sufferer of envy is Narcissus, wasting away while looking upon a reflection he cannot grasp, is in fact an image of his envious brethren.

Yet, the deception of Narcissus implied a further type of blindness. Narcissus was unable to see clearly enough to notice that the image was only a reflection as a result of his curse. His vision could not have been that good. Or, we have a case for what psychologists call 'counter-transference,' when a therapist (or someone who is being projected upon) either projects back on the other some of his own problems or takes on the role that has been projected upon him.[88]

Greeks associated both physical and spiritual blindness with the Evil Eye.[89] Physical anomalies of the eyes, cataracts or even blue eyes were seen as indicative of a dangerous glance. Certainly, spiritual blindness had to be understood when one contemplates the spiritual suffering of the envious. This is witnessed in Sophocles' tragedies of King Oedipus. However, Siebers cleverly asserted that Narcissus' curse is that he saw himself not as he really is but as the Boeotians saw him.[90]

The association with physical anomalies was not necessarily confined to individuals. Both Pliny and Plutarch told fantastic tales of entire peoples or tribes which had the power of *vaskanía*, while Philo contemptuously classifies Egyptians (probably Ptolemaic Greeks) as *baskanon*.[91] To the writers, these people were so full of envy that they destroyed all manner of living things with their eyes. Many sources also attributed the Evil Eye to certain animals.

Avoiding the Evil Eye and Envy

The Greeks appeared no different than most cultures when it came to defensive postures against the Evil Eye. Foster's observations on envy avoidance in peasant culture can clearly be seen in Greek society, both ancient and modern. Other than amulets, peasants will often revert to 'camouflage' to avoid the Evil Eye. This can either be veiling an object from public view[92] (i.e. royalty demanding the averting of eyes or high fences around property) or 'soiling.'[93] The former ensures that envy is not stirred up in the neighbor, and that those already predisposed to envy don't get the opportunity to apply their glance.

The latter is most popular in peasant cultures, where things cannot usually be hidden from prying neighbors. Children will be smeared with dirt or left unbathed, and parents will avoid publicly complimenting their own children. More religious parents may avoid compliments at all to avoid the envy of the gods (or demons), or invoke the name of God during the praise (i.e., 'thank

God!').[94] Children may even be given derogatory nick-names as if to prove parental disdain and thus eliminate any basis for envy.

Compliments are dangerous. They invoke envy, but they can also be signs of enviousness and thus a threat.[95] The envious will not readily admit their malice, and so they compensate by showering the subject of their envy with praise. And so, people refrain from bestowing compliments without invoking the protection of the gods to prove they are not envious. After all, the suspicion of enviousness by others can have dire consequences.

In the interest of appearing uninterested in other's wealth, a peasant will often advertise his own fear of other's envy by covering his belongings with amulets against the Evil Eye.[96] Such public displays of his own fear over his possessions is a way of taking the side of other concerned with their neighbors' envy. If this is not enough, a neighbor may revert to ostentatious consumption or even bragging to prove he has no interest in his neighbors' possessions. This conspicuous consumption would not be considered a threat to the Limited Good of the community if in fact it was obvious to observers that there was little content to the claims.

2

Envy and the Evil Eye in the Old Testament

Fertility and the Unlimited Good of the Old Testament

If we explore Genesis' creation account, we are bound to discover that the pagan notion of fertility as *mana* is utterly refuted by the Scriptures. Our conclusion is that Scripture argues for an *Unlimited Good*. Evil is not created, and creation itself is not described in terms that would allow for evil as part of its design. There is only good, and fertility is part of the very fabric of creation rather than something added to it.

Matthieu Casalis' breakdown of the Creation Epic in terms of P and J documents helps clarify the interplay of fertility issues with Genesis' theology.[97] His comparisons between the P and J narratives and ancient Near Eastern myths are enlightening, but we will confine ourselves strictly to the Biblical text.

The method of creation in P is dysjunction or separation of spaces: light and darkness and especially water from land.[98] The chaotic waters of Genesis 1:2 are tamed and separated so that life can begin as things are placed in order. God also proclaims each thing that He creates (by ordering it out of chaos) to be good. What is most important (and revolutionary) about this story (which Casalis fails to grasp) is that Yahweh did not create the living plants, birds, fish and animals with His hands, but rather *commands* the air, water and earth to put forth creatures. He creates with His words, with a promise. We may think of this in terms of building a theatrical stage. God first assembles the stage from random lumber and installs lighting. On command of the Director, the stage itself spontaneously produces its own props, a wardrobe and backdrops. God's activity is through speech, an important concept for later discussions. The notable exception to this is man, whose creation in both P and J involves the greatest intimacy as Yahweh shapes Adam from the earth and breathes life into his nostrils, something not done to the animals. We note, however, that the ground from which God fashioned Adam was in itself fertile from the beginning.

Fertility is a part of creation, rather than being an unseen force or random luck. To believe the Genesis story is to acknowledge that all of inanimate creation has the potential for producing life so long as God pronounces the *word*. Barrenness and infertility are unnatural, and so man's ancient concern over fertility is overcome by knowing that if things are as God intends them to be there will always be life.[99] Therefore, fertility is not concern for Biblical characters, all of whom eventually sire offspring and are most often blessed large flocks. There is an interesting tale of Jacob trying to influence the marking of his animals, but the text explicitly states that he did not do this to increase the fertility of his flocks (Ge 30:37-43) and that later he even states that the Lord is responsible for his increase over Laban.

This sheds new light on the Exodus themes of manna (this time we mean food!) from heaven and water coming forth from rocks, as well as the various theophanies of God appearing in the desert (c.f. Isaiah). Yahweh reveals the nature of His creation by exposing its natural fertility in places thought to be barren by all appearances. Barrenness itself is not part of God's natural order, but comes into being through man's disobedience and the curse which he brings upon himself and the cosmos (Ge 3:16-19). This accounts for why deserts, which are quite plentiful in the Near East, are not described in the creation epic. Infertility is also linked to the devil (Is 14:17).

The theme running through J[100] is the reason for creation; the description of creation in terms of man. The J story also uses the terms 'garden' and 'soil' to place the various creation events. 'Soil' indicates the raw material of earth, while 'garden' indicates the ecosystem established by Yahweh.[101] When man disobeys the word of Yahweh, he is expelled from the garden, which implies a disruption in the established order. This accounts for the resulting disruption in fertility: the word of God no longer reigns on earth through man's own failure to heed the word.

What the intertwined stories indicate together is that while there is fertility based on how the ecosystem was designed, Yahweh is still capable of preventing life or causing it to take place if He so desires. Yahweh governs the balance of fluids by keeping back the seas and sending rain, but He does not send out "fertility." This is an important change from pagan thought.

Human fertility is revealed in Genesis, since man was shaped by God from this earth which is inherently fertile in the J epic. However, man was especially made by God in His image in the P story. He is not brought forth from the earth as are plants and animals, but he is made especially by God. The implication here is that humanity is a 'limited good' in the text. If man were to be completely wiped out (i.e., the Flood), the earth would not auto-generate more humans as it could plants or animals. This necessitates God's constant intervention on behalf of man to assure his survival.

On the other hand, the rather anti-Darwinian practice of sacrificing one's best in gratitude to God (and to recognize His ownership) is also explained as not being a self-destructive practice. Rather, this showing of gratitude is designed to demonstrate that it is not good breeding practices but God's direct intervention that creates "spotless" animals.

As if to hammer home the 'unlimited good' further into the reader's mind, we must also look at the miracles of the Old Testament. From Abraham until the return from the Babylonian Captivity, God's people have always entered a land already occupied. In terms of 'limited good,' land that is already occupied is off-limits. Ancestral claims of territory are considered permanent in Near East culture as in most other parts of the world. To believe that the ragged band of wanderers will overtake established tribes is unnatural from a 'limited good' perspective, just as the Philistine's reaction to Abraham was entirely predictable: he encroached on established territorial boundaries and upset the balance of the 'limited good.' Yet, somehow the People are able to find room in a land already divided up. We need not bore the reader with a laundry list of the many water and food miracles that reveal the fertility of nature directed by Yahweh.

The Eye in Scripture

In her book *The Evil Eye in the Bible and Rabbinic Literature*, Rikva Ulmer methodically combs the various Talmud and Midrash commentaries for Evil Eye references. Her yield of material is rich, though much of it is heavily influenced by later thought from the post-Captivity and Hellenistic periods which feature the Evil Eye as a magical assault rather than as an ethical disposition. For this reason, we will selectively use rabbinic commentaries (Talmud and Midrash) to discern what passages of Scripture deal specifically with envy and the Evil Eye. Joshua Trachtenberg notes that the *Palestinian Mishna* described the Evil Eye only in terms of moral disposition, while the Babylonian commentaries picked up the rather poorly explained belief in the Evil Eye as a power.[102]

Our first task in our analysis is to turn to the vocabulary used in Scripture to describe the eye itself. The primary word is *ayin*, occurring 376 times either in its root form or in combination with various endings or within names. Its meanings include:

physical eyes
RSV Exodus 21:26 When a man strikes the **eye** (*ayin*) of his slave, male or female, and destroys it, he shall let the slave go free for the **eye's** (*ayin*) sake.

face
Exodus 10:5 and they shall cover the **face** (*ayin*) of the land, so that no one can see the land; and they shall eat what is left to you after the hail, and they shall eat every tree of yours which grows in the field,

mental faculties and awareness
Genesis 3:7 Then the **eyes** (*ayin*) of both were opened, and they knew that they were naked; and they sewed fig leaves together and made themselves aprons.

attitude, intention or emotion
Psalm 17:11 They track me down; now they surround me; they **set their eyes** (*ayin*) to cast me to the ground.

fresh water well or oasis city
Genesis 16:7 The angel of the LORD found her by a **spring** (*ayin*) of water in the wilderness, the spring on the way to Shur.

envy
1 Samuel 18:9 And Saul **eyed** (*ayin*) David from that day on.

What we can see from even the most cursory reading of the Hebrew text is that the concept of 'eye' represents a variety of faculties from the modern perspective. The eyes are the primary means of awareness (c.f. Ex 21:8 and Nu 14:14). Men lift up their faces or heads to see the enemy, but especially the *eyes*. Similarly, to be blinded or to lose an eye is a catastrophic loss.[103] The eye is linked with man's ability to deal with the world (a concept not lost on Plato from our earlier discussion), and to shut the eye is to deny reality. To fully investigate the many colorful uses of eye language in the Hebrew Scripture goes far beyond the scope of this paper, and we ought to alert the reader that the analysis presented here is far from complete.

Our focus will be limited to references to the Evil Eye, such as in:

KJV Deuteronomy 28:54 So that the man that is tender among you, and very delicate, his eye shall be evil (*baskanei to ophthalmo* in the Greek Septuagint, *raa ayin* in Hebrew) toward his brother, and toward the wife of his bosom, and toward the remnant of his children which he shall leave:

The *ra ayin* can only be translated as Evil Eye (the RSV erroneously translates as 'grudge'), which the Septuagint (the rabbinical 3rd century B.C. Greek translation of the Old Testament) translates as *vaskanía*, since *raa* (evil) here and the example below is in the verb form (lit., 'eviling with the eye'). In translating the Septuagint, the rabbis also used 'bad/sick eye' in place of *vaskanía*, which carries the same meaning:

> KJV Deuteronomy 15:9 Beware that there be not a thought in thy wicked heart, saying, The seventh year, the year of release, is at hand; and thine eye be evil (*raa ayin*) against thy poor brother, and thou givest him nought; and he cry unto the LORD against thee, and it be sin unto thee.

This appears at first glance not to be an issue of envy, but rather stinginess. The Scriptures as a whole seem to combine envy with hatred of one's brother,[104] which makes a great deal of sense when one considers that one cannot have either emotion towards one that is truly beloved. We therefore see that the early rabbis understood vaskanía to represent a moral disposition rather than a mystical power.

Such stinginess, according to the Scriptures, will ultimately lead to the brother's death. Envy, which the Greeks defined as the destruction of another for possessing something the envious desires, plays out in biblical thought simply as the desire to possess even if it means the destruction of others (no matter the social rank of the other). The Evil Eyed/envious man is so insidious that the Scriptures warn:

> KJV Proverbs 23:6 Eat thou not the bread of him that hath an evil eye evil (*baskano* in the Greek Septuagint, *raa ayin* in Hebrew), neither desire thou his dainty meats:

> Proverbs 28:22 He that hasteth to be rich hath an evil eye evil (*baskanos* in the Greek Septuagint, *ra ayin* in Hebrew), and considereth not that poverty shall come upon him.

We see how *vaskanía* as enviousness is the primary definition of the Evil Eye in Late Hebrew thought. The envious man is not simply called *phthonos*, but the writer specifically chose a word to invoke the image of assault. Ulmer notes the use of *baskanos* (implying a sorcerer) in Proverbs 28:22 indicated the degree of condemnation associated with this term,[105] and hearkens to our earlier discussions of envy and witchcraft. It might be argued that the Hebrew term *ra ayin* has two different meanings depending on context (e.g., the envious Saul in 1 Samuel 18:9 versus the stinginess in Deuteronomy 15:9), just as "eye" and "well" can both be understood from *ayin*. Envy in the Greek sense is a single symptom of what Hebraic thought categorizes as a greater illness.

Those who are envious or stingy are to be avoided because of their sin (c.f. Wi 1:5 & 6:23-25, Si 21:1 & 14:3 & 37:10, Pr 23:6-8). The most graphic appears again in Sirach:

> RSV Sirach 18:18 A fool is ungracious and abusive, and the gift of a grudging (*baskanou*) man makes the eyes dim.

Here, the gift of the *baskanos* literally "melts" the eyes of the recipient. This image appears in Zechariah 14:12, where the eyes and tongues of those hating Israel will dissolve. This passage implies the assault on Jerusalem described in the text is motivated by envy.

The Law also requires that one have no 'passive' malice (as opposed to a *vaskanía* assault) towards anyone. The condemnation of the man who does not help his brother prevent a loss is abundantly clear in De 22:1-4. This passive malice, by its equal condemnation with stinginess and Evil Eye, is thus a "partner in crime." Those who share company with stingy and envious people endanger themselves.

Ophthalmos poneros (*see De 15:9 above*) is also used to describe the Evil Eye when not separated by *en* (thus, "evil *in* the eye" or "seen as wicked"), *poneros* meaning spoiled, bad or evil.[106] Having explored concepts of vision, we also see the Septuagint Greek use of *en* illuminating the concept of vision by which the image is brought into the viewer's eye. *Ophthalmos poneros* is used by Plato and Hippocrates to describe a physically sick eye,[107] but within Hellenistic Judaism it takes on an additional meaning that we will see used in the New Testament. *Poneros* is also a proper name for Satan (i.e. 'the evil one' in Mt 16:3, 13:19 & 13:38, Jn 17:15). This implies craftiness and scheming, given the devil's history.

Another term used in the Septuagint Apocryphal books is *ophthalomos pleonektos*, or "greedy eye" (Si 14.9). The interplay between *vaskanía* and *ophthalmos poneros* is fascinating in Sirach:

RSV Sirach 14:3 Riches are not seemly for a stingy man; and of what use is property to an envious (*baskano*) man?
:4 Whoever accumulates by depriving himself, accumulates for others; and others will live in luxury on his goods.
:5 If a man is mean (*poneros*) to himself, to whom will he be generous? He will not enjoy his own riches.
:6 No one is meaner (*poneroteros*) than the man who is grudging (*baskainontos*) to himself, and this is the retribution for his baseness;
:7 even if he does good, he does it unintentionally, and betrays his baseness in the end.
...
14:8 Evil (*poneros*) is the man with a grudging eye (*baskainon ophthalmo*); he averts his face and disregards people.
:9 A greedy man's eye is not satisfied with a portion, and mean (*ponera*) injustice withers the soul.
:10 A stingy man's (*phthoneros*) eye (*ophthalmos poneros*) begrudges bread, and it is lacking at his table.
...
31:13 Remember that a greedy eye (*ophthalmos poneros*) is a bad thing. What has been created more greedy than the eye? Therefore it sheds tears from every face.

In Sirach 14:10 we return again to *phthonos*, from our earlier discussion of Greek terminology. Since its appearance is strictly in the Greek Apocryphal texts, we cannot explore its Hebrew equivalent. Though separated in Hellenistic thought, the entanglement of covetousness and envy in Semitic thought survived the linguistic shift in Sirach. *Phthonos* loses its limitation within a class and can obviously be felt towards an inferior.

RSV Tobit 4:7 Give alms from your possessions to all who live uprightly, and do not let your eye begrudge (*phthonesato*) the gift when you make it. Do not turn your face away from any poor man, and the face of God will not be turned away from you.
...
4:16 Give of your bread to the hungry, and of your clothing to the naked. Give all your surplus to charity, and do not let your eye begrudge (*phthonesato*) the gift when you made it.

1 Maccabees 8:16 They trust one man each year to rule over them and to control all their land; they all heed the one man, and there is no envy (*phthonos*) or jealousy (*zelos*) among them.

3 Maccabees 6:7 Daniel, who through envious slanders (*diabolais phthonou*) was cast down into the ground to lions as food for wild beasts, you brought up to the light unharmed.

Wisdom 2:24 but through the devil's envy (*phthono de diabolou*) death entered the world, and those who belong to his party experience it.

In the two quotes from Tobit, we see *poneros* replaced by *phthonos* in its placement with *ophthalmos*, hence "envy" and "evil" are inextricably linked. What is interesting in Tobit is that the envy is aimed downward, an impossibility in Greek thought but not so in Semitic thought. The Maccabees references seem more in keeping with Greek thought, as does Wisdom 6:23.

The envious glance is also described as "eyeing" in Hebrew, "underlooking" (*hypoblepomenos*) in Greek (a possible relationship with the English term to "overlook" as casting the Evil Eye?).

RSV 1 Samuel 18:9 And Saul eyed (*hypoblepomenos* in Greek, *ayin* in Hebrew) David from that day on.

Sirach 37:10 Do not consult the one who looks at you suspiciously (*hypoblepomenou*); hide your counsel from those who are jealous (*zelounton*) of you.

Our final term (mentioned earlier but worth a closer look), which crosses over in both the Old Testament Hebrew text and the Greek version (predominantly in the Apocryphal books) is *vaskanía* itself.

Deuteronomy 28:56 The most tender and delicately bred woman among you, who would not venture to set the sole of her foot upon the ground because she is so delicate and tender, will grudge (*baskanei to ophthalmo* in Septuagint Greek, *raa ayin* in Hebrew) to the husband of her bosom, to her son and to her daughter,
see also De 28:54

We see in the various employments of *vaskanía* in the Septuagint translation of the Hebrew text, all correlate to *ra ayin*. Along with the references to *vaskanía* already cited (Si 14:3-14, Pr 23:6 & 28:22, De 28:54-56), there are several other occurrences:

RSV Wisdom 4:12 For the fascination (*baskania*) of wickedness obscures what is good, and roving desire perverts the innocent mind.

4 Maccabees 1:26 In the soul it is boastfulness, covetousness, thirst for honor, rivalry, and malice (*baskania*);

4 Maccabees 2:15 It is evident that reason rules even the more violent emotions: lust for power, vainglory, boasting, arrogance, and malice (*baskanias*).

Sirach 37:11 Do not consult with a woman about her rival or with a coward about war, with a merchant about barter or with a buyer about selling, with a grudging man (*baskanou*) about gratitude or with a merciless man about kindness, with an idler about any work or with a man hired for a year about completing his work, with a lazy servant about a big task—pay no attention to these in any matter of counsel.

These four remaining citations of *vaskanía* can be understood with the classical Greek (non-magical) meaning we discussed earlier. In Wisdom 4:12, we see *vaskanía* as fascination or hypnosis, in this case with evil. This sounds the same as Cicero's warning against contemplating something too closely, as doing so will incite envy and desire. Both of the 4 Maccabees citations list *vaskanía* much in the same way we understand envy in Greek mythology. Covetousness is mentioned separately here whereas elsewhere it appears as a simile to *vaskanía*, its inclusion in the list appears to be an attempt to lump various words for the same depravity rather than drawing out semantic differences. The final citation in Sirach 37:11 is interesting because gratitude is antithetical to *vaskanía*.

We must therefore conclude that the Evil Eye is a moral disposition towards self-centeredness and thus evil conduct. The Evil Eye is a failure to share with those in need, thus a withholding of God's blessings from others and causing death through broken communion between the suffering and God.

The Eye of Mishpat and Hospitality

On the opposite side is the "good eye," which is generous and loving towards the neighbor (c.f. Proverbs 22:9—"He who has a bountiful [good] eye (*tov ayin*) will be blessed, for he shares his bread with the poor."). This word *tov* is the same 'good' that Yahweh pronounces over each day of creation. Bountifulness and good in creation are reflections of God's generosity and goodness.

Sirach 31:12-31 is concerned with appropriate table manners when receiving another's God-mandated hospitality. Since Yahweh legislated hospitality, the Lord's food is at the host's table. In verse 13, one is told to weep over everything with tears of gratitude. The eye that does not weep is not grateful for the bounty provided by God and is naturally envious.

Hospitality, described as a 'good eye,' is the ultimate sign that one believes in the Unlimited Good of God. As a rule, those who are faithful to Yahweh are generous towards others, knowing that God will always provide enough good if they follow the Law. We will speak of hospitality as sharing with another, differentiating this from sharing with God, which is sacrifice.

The motivation behind hospitality is that God sees it (Ze 4:10), according to rabbinical commentaries.[108] Rashi, the medieval rabbinic commentator, explains that Torah deals more harshly with a thief (c.f. Ex 22:2-8 & De 24:7) than a robber because the former commits his crime while completely disregarding God as witness to it, whereas a robber does his crime knowing that God and men are both watching. The thief's higher regard for the eyes of men than of God makes his crime all the worse, a practice repeatedly condemned in Scripture (c.f. Is 29:15, Ez 8:12 & Ps 94:7).[109] This magnifies the crime of Cain, who thought that God would not see his murder.

Abraham's well-known act of hospitality to the angelic visitors (Genesis 18) became the subject of one of the most popular icons in the Orthodox Church, but the Scriptures have more to say about Abraham. Our previous discussion of Abraham showed him to be righteous not only through his belief in God but dealings with Hagar and Ishmail. Because of the promise of God to bless the whole world through Abraham's seed, the rabbis have a unique interpretation of Genesis 14. Verse 7 says: "And they returned, and came to Enmishpat, which is Kadesh, and smote all the country of the Amalekites, and also the Amorites, that dwelt in Hazezontamar (RSV)." This is an attack upon the land in which Abraham dwells, thus the invading kings posed a threat to Abraham and his community. *Enmishpat* literally means 'Eye (or Well) of Justice' and *kadesh* is a mismarking of *kodesh*, which means 'holy.' The rabbis saw the attack as an assault on God's holy Eye of Justice, which looked down upon Abraham as the source of God's justice (i.e. mercy and hospitality) to the world (c.f. Ge 18:19).[110] Therefore, those who claim to be inheritors of Abraham's blessing must likewise practice Abraham's hospitality, something Christ will remind the Jews of in the Gospels. The definition of a son of Abraham is his practice of hospitality and mercy.

The Moabites, on the other hand, are envious and unjust: they are the same tribe that later refused to feed Israel (i.e. act hospitably) during the Exodus from Egypt. This story also explains the later appearance of Melchizedek and the tithe

to Yahweh, as well as Abraham's care not to plunder what his men had retrieved
of Sodom and Gomorrah's wealth.

The revelation of God's *mishpat* or justice is the Torah:

> RSV Deuteronomy 10:17 For the LORD your God is God of gods and Lord
> of lords, the great, the mighty, and the terrible God, who is not partial and
> takes no bribe.
> :18 He executes justice (*mishpat*) for the fatherless and the widow, and loves
> the sojourner, giving him food and clothing.
> :19 Love the sojourner therefore; for you were sojourners in the land of Egypt.
> :20 You shall fear the LORD your God; you shall serve him and cleave to him,
> and by his name you shall swear.
> :21 He is your praise; he is your God, who has done for you these great and
> terrible things which your eyes have seen.
> :22 Your fathers went down to Egypt seventy persons; and now the LORD
> your God has made you as the stars of heaven for multitude.
>
> Deuteronomy 16:19 You shall not pervert justice (*mishpat*); you shall not
> show partiality; and you shall not take a bribe, for a bribe blinds the eyes of
> the wise and subverts the cause of the righteous.
> :20 Justice, and only justice, you shall follow, that you may live and inherit the
> land which the LORD your God gives you.
> *See also Ex 33:19, De 24:17 & 27:19.*

The previous citation should make the connection between mercy and justice
clear. Israel is called to show hospitality not only to its own members but also the
stranger or foreigner. In Exodus, the center of cultic worship is the 'mercy seat,'
which sits upon the broken tablets of the Law. Yahweh expects Israel to be merciful in His sight, lest He withhold from them rain and they perish (De 13). Israel
is also mentioned as the "apple" of God's eye Zechariah 2:12, which can either
mean God's love for Israel or that God's mercy (which He gives according to
what He sees) is centered on Israel.[111]

Aside from tears of gratitude, what else comes out of the eye? The answer
should be clear: *mishpat*. God's vision is directly linked in the Scriptures to His
action. A good eye means that the person looking through it will do the compas-
sionate works commanded by God. Good things will enter his eye (i.e. he will see
God's blessings and be moved to gratitude), and he will be merciful and just
towards those he sees (i.e. things will pass out of his eye or judgement/rational
faculties). The envious man with his narrow eye sees no good, since good cannot
enter his eye (i.e. his eye does not see God's blessings). Neither can the good
works of the Law exit his eye (i.e. he cannot be moved to *mishpat* by seeing God's

blessings). His eye is 'choked off' since the outcome of his vision is stinginess. What comes out are curses, to the extent that even the gifts he gives and the food the envious one shares is evil and poisonous. The Good Eye and the Evil Eye are thus moral dispositions rather than magical powers, and vision is inextricably linked to morality.

Ulmer lists various rabbinic attributes to the eye: *'ayin ra'ah* ("evil eye"), *'ayin tovah* ("good eye" or generosity), *'ayin yafah* ("beautiful eye" or goodwill) and *'ayin tsarah* ("narrow eye" or stinginess).[112] The eyes divulge the intentions of the other. Lest we forget our previous discussion of eye emanations vis-à-vis Plato and Euclid, we see the very ancient concept of the eyes radiating light attested to in the dimming eyes (in Hebrew, literally to grow heavy or dark) of Isaac, Israel and Elijah (Ge 27:1, 48:10 & 1 Sa 3:2). The great liveliness of Moses is spoken of as his eyes not dimming despite his age (De 34:7). While these verses may refer to physical eyesight, they may also imply slowness of judgement (in Genesis 21, Isaac is deceived by Jacob in a crude attempt to impersonate Esau, which Isaac almost doesn't fall for).

Only the first two eye terms appear in Scripture (Good Eye and Evil Eye). The latter are hinted at. The beautiful eye is mentioned in Jeremiah 3:40, when the prophet condemns Israel as a woman who paints her eye to appear larger and thus more attractive. A large eye is valued as beautiful, so we can assume that a small or narrow eye is undesirable. If *mishpat* is projected from the eye (in terms of words and merciful actions), then a beautiful eye would be large while an Evil Eye would be narrow. The latter would be less likely to see goodness in others, nor allow acts of righteousness to pass outwards.

So, how can we then understand the Hebrew understanding of eyesight? While the Hebrews did seem to have some belief in light in the eyes (c.f. Ge 27:1, 48:10), the consistent use of the term "in" (c.f. 1Ki 11:38, Is 48:4, Ge 34:11) both in Hebrew and Septuagint Greek to denote eyesight shows the primary emphasis on the image entering the eye and having an effect on the viewer. Such terms as "what is good/evil in your eyes" often appear, when the viewer is asked to render judgement over the image that has come into his eyes. This makes vision itself a passive experience when compared to the Greek notion of visual rays.

In the modern understanding of vision, once light has struck the eye and the image is transferred to the visual cortex of the brain, the "signal" (i.e. image) is split to the limbic system (which governs the emotional reaction) and the neocortical system (higher intellectual functions including physical response). Without getting into much detail, the limbic reaction is much faster and longer lasting than the neocortical response, since the latter deals with more information and essentially programs the limbic system on how to immediately react. We suggest the Biblical understanding of vision is a reflection of this process. The limbic response assigns an immediate value to a visual signal (i.e., when sin approaches, it is "good in my eyes"), while the neocortical system assigns a higher value and response (i.e., "I should not do this because God says it is evil" or "It is wrong for me to feel this way"). Later, with enough proper neocortical responses, the limbic system learns to respond appropriately (i.e., it is now "evil in my eyes"). The spiritual life then is governed by gaining control of the neocortical areas of the brain and then reprogramming the limbic system.

The limbic connection or the expectation of strong emotion when one sees something, appears to be behind the use of "upon" with the eyes. In each case of its occurrence, the viewer anticipates certain emotions or expectations:

> KJV Genesis 39:7 And it came to pass after these things, that his master's wife cast her eyes upon Joseph; and she said, Lie with me.
> See also Ge 44:21, 2 Sa 22:28, Jb 16:9, Ps 34:15, Ps 101:6 & Ps 145:15

There is certainly no sign of the Greek understanding of visual rays in the use of "upon." To clarify this point, we see the use of upon in terms of an emotional expectation if the eye is laid upon the object being seen rather than an eye emanation.

> KJV Psalm 54:7 For he hath delivered me out of all trouble: and mine eye hath seen his desire upon mine enemies.

> Ezekiel 24:16 Son of man, behold, I take away from thee the desire of thine eyes with a stroke: yet neither shalt thou mourn nor weep, neither shall thy tears run down.

> Ecclesiastes 6:9 Better is the sight of the eyes than the wandering of the desire: this is also vanity and vexation of spirit.

If there is no emanation from the eye, but rather the condition of the eye leads to a certain type of ethical behavior (e.g., a word), then we can better understand Judaism reliance on texts as "amulets" against the Evil Eye. Archeology and historical collections have revealed a wide array of talismans employed by the Jews against the Evil Eye. The concept behind text amulets, we believe, is that they purposely carry the word of God into the desirous eye. The viewer is reminded of

God's words, and responds either by checking his envy or changing his target. Word and vision are linked, in that the word is a revelation of how one sees the world (moral disposition).

The evidence of the Fall of man and his fallen moral disposition (thus an Evil Eye) is in fact man's speech. When Adam and Eve's eyes were opened in the Garden and they saw their nakedness (Gen 3:6-7), they both began to accuse each other and the serpent (Gen 3:12-13). The accusation is a manifestation of guilt, which can be directly paralleled to our prior discussion of the witchcraft and Evil Eye accusations associated with envy. Sieber's observation of the projection of one's sins onto a target (like Narcissus) occurs here with Adam and Eve as they try to blame each other and thus transfer guilt.

As a theme running through the Old Testament, we see the "narrow eye" of men and their resulting evil words juxtapose to the "good eye" of Yahweh and His merciful words. Psalm 50:14-21 demonstrates the link between seeing and evil words. Ezekiel 22:9 directly links slander to murder. In Numbers 14:36, the spies Moses sends out return from seeing the Promised Land only to "slander" Moses and Yahweh, a rejection of God's benevolent gift to the people of Israel. Here we see the spies adhering to the Limited Good (the land being already occupied, thus no room for Israel), thus believing that God cannot provide anything more for them. We will later see a connection between the Evil Eye and the Exodus theme.

Envy and the Law

For a most telling discussion of the envy concept in Scripture, we must turn to the Decalog, which is the root of God's condemnation of man's sin and is central to the Books of Moses. Louis Smith analyzed the Decalog,[113] appearing in both Exodus 20 and Deuteronomy 5, in terms of a chiasm. Chiasm is a well-documented literary form which frequently appears in both the Old and New Testaments,[114] in which a series of statements lead to a conclusion, followed by a series of points parallel to the first set of statements. After combining the first two commandments (no gods before Yahweh and no idols), Smith centers the chiasm on the sixth commandment. Below is a simple chart according to Smith's analysis:[115]

E
Thou shalt not kill (6)

D Honor thy parents (5)   (7) Do not commit adultery **D'**

C Remember the Sabbath (4)   (8) Do not steal **C'**

B Care for the Lord's Name (3)   (9) Care for neighbor's name **B'**

A No idolatry (1/2)   (10) No coveting **A'**

Figure 1.1—Decalog Breakdown According to Louis Smith

At E, we see the central purpose of the commandments: to preserve human life from self-destruction. The violation of the Law, by this analysis, ultimately results in death. God's reason for giving the Law is to be found in De 6:2-3:

> KJV Deuteronomy 6:2 That thou mightest fear the LORD thy God, to keep all his statutes and his commandments, which I command thee, thou, and thy son, and thy son's son, all the days of thy life; and that thy days may be prolonged.
> :3 Hear therefore, O Israel, and observe to do it; that it may be well with thee, and that ye may increase mightily, as the LORD God of thy fathers hath promised thee, in the land that floweth with milk and honey.

The D and C levels of the chiasm are obvious parallels, having to do with respecting social order and property against envy assaults. Since the Lord presents Himself as the Bridegroom and Father to His people, these commandments apply to human relations with the Almighty as well as with other humans.

B and B' represent care for the Name of the Lord as well as the neighbor. It should be obvious that one who cannot honor another will certainly have a hard time with the other. Recalling our earlier discussion of envy, we can see this commandment set as a direct prohibition of the gossip and slander often associated with peasant village life and envious behavior. This is also a remedy to the witchcraft accusations that surfaced in our discussion of envy from a sociological perspective. By equating the neighbor's good name with the Lord's, the gossip and slanderer offends the good name of God. Furthermore, it is a biblical principle that slander leads to bloodshed (Ez 22:9, Le 19:6, Sr 26:5 & 28:14).

The chiasm begins and ends with what initially seem to be utterly divorced concepts: idolatry and covetousness (c.f. Co 3:5). Smith concludes that covetousness is the desiring of that which was not promised by God, and turning to idols who promise the things God does not.[116] While this is plausible, this paper argues that the specific promises of God have nothing to do with covetousness. God promises life to those who obey the Law in terms of laws of nature (i.e. to violate the Law is to violate the created order rather than randomly selected prohibitions), and death for those who break the Law by violating the order of creation. The Lord does not threaten to execute law-breakers, but men simply die by breaking the Law in violation of their nature.

The careful reader will see that if everything belongs to the Creator, then to believe that one *deserves* something is in fact *self-idolatry*. This is the rejection of God. Smith's argument that idols promise men things is in fact a delusion: the idols are made by men, men who then attribute promises to the idols (c.f. Is 48:5 & 46:7).

What this also shows us is that murder is the final result of violating the Law, just as no violation of the Law can occur without one first being an idolater. The Decalog shows the dynamic that idolatry leads to envy, which leads to murder. If one is perfectly oriented towards God, one cannot sin. Only in a minor deviation, in a slight preference aside from God, is one idolatrous and capable of sin. This slight preference for one's self instead of God reveals that one deserves something more than God is the seed of envy. Envy ultimately relies on *self-deserving*.

This is the primary biblical context of envy, something the Greeks were never able to grasp in their analyses. Greeks naturally understood individuals as units of self, turned inward towards their own existence. The self is primary, and the favor of the gods was solicited for the sustenance of the self. If the self is primary, then the self deserves everything that it can get. The Bible does not argue from a human-self point of view, but argues a thoroughly theocentric worldview in which mankind is in fact deserving of nothing. The deceit of Adam and Eve was their own belief that they *deserved* to eat of the Tree. Their awakening from their delusion came with the onset of death, when their inward turning selfishness tore the very fabric of their being from communion with God.

No matter how self-deserving envy is acted out, the violation always ends in the bloodshed of death. We may say that the reason God does not execute the Law-breaker is that the one who violates the Law in effect executes himself. The tearing away from God is self-destruction.

If this is the operating principle, then the only end to any sin is blood. We do not often see our sins as being idolatrous, but the Law clearly shows that the results of sin is death. We can therefore assume that people are not capable of seeing the dynamic of sin until it has accomplished its "natural cycle." Basically, we cannot see the true horror of our violation of the Law until a murder is committed. Once we see blood (even if it is another's), we know the full extent to which we have executed ourselves.

Of course, we would expect that if the Decalog should put forth such a concept, that other parts of the Bible would also reflect this same triangle of idolatry, envy and murder. Aside from the Prophetic passages previously cited, we can also look to Genesis to prove our theory.

Our primary example is that of Cain and Abel (Ge 4:1-16). First, one should notice that while Abel offered the firstlings of his flock, Cain offered some vegetables with no particular significance (i.e., rather than his "biggest" or "best" fruits). Cain's offering shows no sacrifice, unlike his brother's. Yet, Cain also becomes angry when the Lord does not regard his offering. Here we see Cain's selfish idolatry in his keeping the best for himself (which is actually due the Lord because He made the ground the vegetables came from), and then expecting the Lord to praise him for his half-hearted offering!

Cain then slays his brother, and in this we see the first story of men outside Paradise. We see a continuation of man's evil words, this time when the first direct quote of Cain is a lie. He claims not to know his brother's whereabouts after the murder. Yahweh proclaims the curse Cain brought upon himself for his crime, after which Cain cries out knowing the extent of his crime and the horror it will bring to his community. Yahweh's merciful Eye (which we will discuss shortly) is witnessed in His marking of Cain so that he will not be hunted down.

We also see an immediate need for the Law here, which only comes later in the Penteteuch. Adam and Eve's coveting of the fruit (i.e., their desire to become as God without God, a form of idolatry), plays out with their sons. Adam and Eve see their sins in the expulsion, but it is with Cain and Abel that we see the need for blood in order to repent.

Envy Tales in Genesis

We have seen thus far the Scriptural terminology for the Evil Eye and envy, along with a few isolated incidents or warnings. Our belief is that envy continues to surface throughout the Old Testament as a continuous theme and reveals the idolatry of man. We will take only a few examples here to enforce this argument; it will be left to the reader to do further readings of Scripture on his own to see this pattern.

So it is that Abram's fear of the Egyptian's covetousness leads him to deny that Sarai is his wife (Ge 12:11-13). But the stronger envy story centers on Sarai and

Hagar. Sarai asks Abraham to sleep with his Egyptian servant to produce off-spring that Sarai is unable to bear him. However, when Hagar becomes pregnant, Sarah finds herself being "eyed" by Hagar:

> RSV Genesis 16:4 And he went in to Hagar, and she conceived; and when she saw that she had conceived, she looked with contempt (*ayin*) on her mistress.

The Hebrew text uses "eyed," which the Septuagint translates as "shamed her by looking upon (her) in judgement." In modern terms it is to "look down upon," but this is also the Semitic understanding of covetousness. Rather than joyfully sharing her fertility with Sarah (knowing that the first-born son is in fact God's to begin with), Hagar shames the barren Sarai with her gaze. This same phrase is repeated in the next verse, when Sarai complains to Abram, who in turn opts to stay out of the fray. What comes next is another "eyeing:"

> RSV Genesis 16:6 But Abram said to Sarai, "Behold, your maid is in your power; do to her as you please." Then Sarai dealt harshly with her, and she fled from her.

Abram actually asks Sarai to do what is "good in her eyes" (rather than 'as you please') in Hebrew, which the Septuagint translates as "proper" or "pleasing." In Hebrew, the term *tov* is used (the same word Yahweh pronounces at the end of each day of creation in Genesis), a hint that Abram is asking Sarai to be generous. Essentially, Sarai is being challenged by Abram to use her Good Eye towards the woman under her control.[117] Instead, Sarai 'browbeats' Hagar (the Hebrew term is *ayah*, a derivative of 'eye'), which was understood by rabbinic scholars as the Evil Eye.

Though she returns to the camp, Sarai's Evil Eye against Hagar (and Ishmael) continues. Midrash makes a point of explaining that the angelic announcement of Hagar's pregnancy *to come* in the wilderness (Ge 16:11) and the earlier statement of having *already* conceived (Ge 16:4) are in fact two separate pregnancies.[118] The first pregnancy, the scholars believe, was lost due to Sarah's Evil Eye on Hagar. Further evidence for this is Sarah's invocation of God's judgement (Ge 16:5), ostensibly between her and Abraham but actually between her and Hagar's infant from the first conception. Rabbis disagree with the vowel marking making the statement "between me and you (*uveneikha*)," and claim that the vowel markers should make it read "between me and your son (*uvinkha*)."[119] The second pregnancy is a mercy from God upon Hagar for being trapped into such a terrible situation (Ge 16:11).

By the time Hagar flees the second time in Genisis 21:14-16, Ishmael (by this time in his twenties according to various Midrash commentators) is so afflicted that he is no longer able to walk.[120] While his exact age is unknown, before Isaac was born, Ishmael was circumcised with Abraham at 13 years of age. Accounting for whatever time transpired between the circumcision, Isaac's birth and the voice of God permitting Hagar to leave the camp, we know that he should have been able to walk by himself rather than needing to be carried by his mother. His inability to walk is explained by the rabbis as affliction with the Evil Eye,[121] and God's mercy intervenes to allow Ishmael to escape before the oppression costs him his life.

Abraham's obedience in Genesis 22 is an example of his respect for God's right to his first-born as is later outlined in the Law given in Exodus. Abraham does not have a "narrow eye" but remains obedient knowing that God will provide for him (Ge 22:7). Fr. Paul Tarazi, when discussing this topic,[122] observed that the very name of the place where Yahweh proclaims the future conception of Ishmail is called Beerlahairoi or the "well of the living one seeing me" (which does not use the root *ayin* for 'well,' so it is not a play on words), again a link between seeing and proclamation of the word. Hagar then says that Yahweh has seen her because He spoke mercifully to her. It may be implied that Yahweh blessed Hagar because she trusted in God's Good Eye. Sarah never repents of her enviousness, quite possibly because she never sees the death of Ishmail. Had he died from her Evil Eye, the story would probably have come out much different.

Isaac came to fear the envy of others, which led him to deny that Rebekah was his wife in Gerar of the Philistines Ge 26:6).

> RSV Genesis 26:14-15 He had possessions of flocks and herds, and a great household, so that the Philistines envied (*qanah/ezelosan*) him. Now the Philistines had stopped and filled with earth all the wells which his father's servants had dug in the days of Abraham his father.

We see *ezelosan* (from the root *zelos* as discussed earlier) in the Septuagint, which translates the Hebrew *qanah* or 'envy.'[123] This is the first occurrence of this Hebrew word for envy in the canonical order of books. *Qanah* is a mixed word, often appearing as *zelos*, but also (as in the case above) representing *phthonos* in the Septuagint Greek translation. Its meaning can only be clarified through context. Here we can see the accuracy of the RSV's use of 'envied,' being that the

Philistines are motivated to commit the highly destructive act of filling wells. After all, wells are a source of life, and by filling them the Philistines are harming not only Isaac, but in the long run themselves. Such self-destructive behavior is clearly indicative of the Philistines' great envy of Abraham.

Confirming our earlier discussion of *zelos* as a mixed term, we see here that *zelos* can either be the envy of the Philistines or the great love of God for His people:

> RSV Exodus 20:5 you shall not bow down to them or serve them; for I the LORD your God am a jealous (*qanah/zelotes*) God, visiting the iniquity of the fathers upon the children to the third and the fourth generation of those who hate me,
> *See also Nu 25:13, Ze 8:2 & De 32:21.*

God is entitled to be jealous for Israel because there is only *one* Israel. To Yahweh, there are no others with which He has a covenant, and thus the only Limited Goods presented in the Bible are God Himself and His people. All other things are part of the Unlimited Good that the Old Testament presents.

Scapegoating and Exodus

We believe that there is a thematic connection between the observed social behavior of peasants in an envy-rich environment with the concept of Exodus as presented by Fr. Paul Tarazi. In short, Tarazi explains that the vision of God, or theophany, is through an Exodus event patterned after Israel's sojourn in the desert at Kadesh-barnea.[124] All of the Penteteuch visions of Yahweh after Adam and Eve occur during a journey, and are defined both by God seeing those in Exodus and visa-versa.[125] A proper list of such visions and the places named after these theophanies is to be found in Tarazi's book, and our interest here is not in enumerating these events but casting them in light of the circumstances surrounding Exodus.

It is our belief that the primary motivation for Exodus is envy. It is envy that initiates and keeps the Exodus in motion, making peace impossible until Yahweh has revealed Himself. Of course, we are not talking about the envy of those in Exodus, but rather the peoples surrounding those in Exodus. These envious and inhospitable nations project their enviousness on those in Exodus and drive them from the land. We have already gone into considerable detail regarding the human trait of projecting community guilt upon an individual, mostly through the act of accusation. Accusation is Adam and Eve's first verbalization as recorded in Genesis, but to look for a clear case of projection in the Old Testament we must look to a different passage:

> KJV Leviticus 16:8-22 And Aaron shall cast lots upon the two goats; one lot for the LORD, and the other lot for the scapegoat. And Aaron shall bring the goat upon which the LORD'S lot fell, and offer him for a sin offering. But the goat, on which the lot fell to be the scapegoat, shall be presented alive before the LORD, to make an atonement with him, and to let him go for a scapegoat into the wilderness…Then shall he kill the goat of the sin offering, that is for the people, and bring his blood within the veil, and do with that blood as he did with the blood of the bullock, and sprinkle it upon the mercy seat, and before the mercy seat…And when he hath made an end of reconciling the holy place, and the tabernacle of the congregation, and the altar, he shall bring the live goat: And Aaron shall lay both his hands upon the head of the live goat, and confess over him all the iniquities of the children of Israel, and all their transgressions in all their sins, putting them upon the head of the goat, and shall send him away by the hand of a fit man into the wilderness: And the goat shall bear upon him all their iniquities unto a land not inhabited: and he shall let go the goat in the wilderness.

After having made atonement for the sins of the people, after which we can assume that God has forgiven their iniquity (i.e., the violation of the Law), we see this strange cultic act. The sins for which there has already been a sacrifice are now laid upon the scapegoat. Why is this? Are we to assume that the sins are not forgiven?

If the cycle of the Decalog is idolatry, envy/covetousness and finally murder, then the Law is designed to complete the cycle of bloodshed with an animal rather than a human being. If the animal sacrifice is not made, men cannot see the wickedness of their deeds and thus those sins not immediately resulting in bloodshed cannot be repented of. The bloodshed of the sacrifice is necessary for men to realize that their sins are leading them on a path to murder. For murder of a man there is no sacrifice (c.f. Nu 35:16-31, Ge 9:5-6 & Ps 51:16), but only execution. Blood has been shed, and the fullness of one's idolatry has been revealed.

According to Scripture God does not enjoy sacrifices for sin (c.f. Ps 40:6, Is 1:11-18 & Ps 51:16-17). In cases where Yahweh enjoys the smoke of sacrifice, it is in the repentance or thanksgiving of the one sacrificing (c.f. Ps 50). What other purpose can there be to sacrifice if it is not to teach men the real consequences of their sins and confess them before the Lord?

If we have such a pedagogical understanding of sacrifice, then we can better comprehend the second goat, the scapegoat. This goat bares men's other sins: slander and accusation, sins in which men have already caused bloodshed and there is no atonement. It represents those of the community already driven out to perish, or a warning as to what can be expected.

The goat is innocent, but the offenses of the community are laid upon it and it is driven into the wilderness to die. Outside of the camp, the goat is subject to dying of thirst or becoming food for predators, whereas before he was safe under the guard of the shepherds. It will only be through God's mercy that the goat will survive. The scapegoat and the sacrificial goat are parallel murders. One is openly bloody while the second is decidedly more subtle.

Our evidence for this interpretation is that both the priest and the man who leads the goat into the wilderness must ritually bathe after handling the scapegoat, just as they must after handling the sacrificed goat. This implies the scapegoat is holy, since both men have been defiled by touching the scapegoat and must be cleansed. It is a sacrifice and yet it lives. Rather, it is a messenger, a topic we will cover a little later.

We may now return to the Exodus theme. How is it that the Exodus has a connection to the scapegoat? Looking closely at the Exodus story, we see that there is more to it than simply God enticing one to pick up camp and head into the bush. Israel was ambivalent about God leading them into the desert considering the amount of grumbling that went on throughout the forty years of sojourning. Israel left because of the greediness of Pharaoh, manifested in his enormous building project. The burden for this was laid on Israel, a type of transference by the Egyptians of their greed onto the 'unlucky' Semites sojourning along the Nile.

We believe that the event of scapegoating is negative reinforcement that God uses to entice people into the Exodus journey. In Egypt, Pharaoh's greed placed a heavy burden upon Israel. Abraham before them came from a land of unrighteousness (after all, he is the only one in his father's land whom God calls righteous!) and continued to move on after each negative encounter along the way to the Promised Land. Jacob also encountered the envy of the Philistines so that he must move on. Finally, Israel was taken into captivity by the rapacious Babylonians.

Tarazi argues that the positive enticement is not only the promises of a better life for the one in Exodus but also the experience of theophany.[126] Yahweh is the God of Exodus, a delivering God. Scapegoating, the act of placing the burdens of the community's sins upon one and being driven out into the wilderness, makes such deliverance possible. Yahweh then saved you not only from the desert you were marching into and made you a people by calling you out of the chaos of the old country, but He lifted the burden which has been imposed on you by the other.

Fallen men do not necessarily find theophany alone an irresistible offering. This is proven by the rather mediocre reaction of the Israelites to their spectacular rescue from Egypt and the Pillar of Fire and Smoke. Certainly the Israelites knew that their journey would take them into the desert, a place of death. For a Semite to leave the *wadi* and journey out into the wilderness was risky because the desert is a place of dryness and death. To those who remained in the safety of the community, the one who went into Exodus was marching straight into the waiting arms of death. Israel's bitter complaints when water could not be found demonstrates that they too were uncertain whether this march was for their survival or execution. However, Israel also knew that there was no going back to Egypt: they had been driven out as scapegoats because of Egypt's greed.

So Yahweh uses a "carrot and stick" method to move people: a burden of projected sin makes it impossible to remain where one is (the stick) and the promise of Paradise for those who follow Him (the carrot). To the one without faith (who cannot imagine Paradise or God's providence), it seems like a dismal proposal either way, since the 'carrot' in this case involves a march through the desert. It is only through faith, particularly the faith as outlined in the Scriptures, that one can expect Yahweh to reveal the natural goodness and fertility of His creation even in the desert. This explains not only the manna from the skies, but the various water episodes: springs gushing forth from the "waters below" or the Red Sea parting, which certainly hearkens back to the Genesis and Flood myths.[127]

Being mindful of Tarazi's proof that one only meets God in Exodus, we may then conclude that it is only by enduring the burden of another's sins that we can be motivated to make an Exodus. This motivation is needed for salvation, which provides a context for God's offer. If men are not aware that they need salvation, how then can God offer it to them and they in turn accept it? Furthermore, does this not essentially agree with the work of the Cross?

In terms of the Evil Eye, it could be said those who are being persecuted and accused are in a different (and possibly closer) relationship to God than those 'in authority' or with wealth. The widows and orphans who are assumed to be envious of those with whole families and financial stability are in fact doubly blessed: they are the focus of the justice of the Law and they are reliant upon God's mercy through which they can meet Him face to face as did Hagar.

There is a certain of degree guilt associated with the one going into Exodus. There are certainly no innocent parties. Adam and Eve rebelled, Cain murdered Abel, Abraham feared jealous murder by foreign kings over Sarah (Isaac had the same problem with Rebekah), Hagar haughtily eyed Sarah, Jacob ripped off the slow-witted (and, later, patently evil) Esau, Joseph bragged to his envious brothers, etc. Men cannot say that that God forced them into being dependent on God's mercy. But, like the sacrifice in place of the murder, God allows men to taste enough of their sin to cry out for salvation rather than face immediate death.

We can then establish a specific Scapegoat/Exodus pattern for the characters in Torah:

1. God sets person aside (Ordination)
2. Person sins (Revelation of weakness & vulnerability)
3. Person receives unjust accusation of community (out of Envy)
4. Burden of community's sins laid upon one (Scapegoat)
5. Person driven into place of death (Exodus)
6. God rescues and blesses (Theophany)

Figure 2.1—Scapegoat/Exodus Pattern in Penteteuch

Obviously, Adam and Eve's tale does have the exception: they blame one another, and so one another's sins are laid upon each other in their accusations. However, overlaying this framework on the various major stories of the Penteteuch will help the reader see the repeated pattern. It is our contention that envy plays a major role in each story, as the Scapegoat becomes the bearer of the community's envy.

The Prophetic Representations of Envy

There are two major addresses of envy in the Old Testament. The first we shall discuss occurs in Numbers. Here we see that a "spirit of jealousy (*ruah qinah*)" or suspicion overtakes (either rightly or wrongly) a husband. Knowing what we do already about the power of envy and jealousy, this emotion is singled out for special attention:

> RSV Numbers 5:1-31 The LORD said to Moses,… "Say to the people of Israel, If any man's wife goes astray and acts unfaithfully against him, if a man lies with her carnally, and it is hidden from the eyes of her husband, and she is

undetected though she has defiled herself, and there is no witness against her, since she was not taken in the act; and if the spirit of jealousy comes upon him, and he is jealous of his wife who has defiled herself; or if the spirit of jealousy comes upon him, and he is jealous of his wife, though she has not defiled herself; then the man shall bring his wife to the priest, and bring the offering required of her, a tenth of an ephah of barley meal; he shall pour no oil upon it and put no frankincense on it, for it is a cereal offering of jealousy, a cereal offering of remembrance, bringing iniquity to remembrance. "And the priest shall bring her near, and set her before the LORD; and the priest shall take holy water in an earthen vessel, and take some of the dust that is on the floor of the tabernacle and put it into the water. And the priest shall set the woman before the LORD, and unbind the hair of the woman's head, and place in her hands the cereal offering of remembrance, which is the cereal offering of jealousy. And in his hand the priest shall have the water of bitterness that brings the curse. Then the priest shall make her take an oath, saying, 'If no man has lain with you, and if you have not turned aside to uncleanness, while you were under your husband's authority, be free from this water of bitterness that brings the curse. But if you have gone astray, though you are under your husband's authority, and if you have defiled yourself, and some man other than your husband has lain with you, then' (let the priest make the woman take the oath of the curse, and say to the woman) 'the LORD make you an execration and an oath among your people, when the LORD makes your thigh fall away and your body swell; may this water that brings the curse pass into your bowels and make your body swell and your thigh fall away.' And the woman shall say, 'Amen, Amen.'

"Then the priest shall write these curses in a book, and wash them off into the water of bitterness; and he shall make the woman drink the water of bitterness that brings the curse, and the water that brings the curse shall enter into her and cause bitter pain. And the priest shall take the cereal offering of jealousy out of the woman's hand, and shall wave the cereal offering before the LORD and bring it to the altar; and the priest shall take a handful of the cereal offering, as its memorial portion, and burn it upon the altar, and afterward shall make the woman drink the water. And when he has made her drink the water, then, if she has defiled herself and has acted unfaithfully against her husband, the water that brings the curse shall enter into her and cause bitter pain, and her body shall swell, and her thigh shall fall away, and the woman shall become an execration among her people. But if the woman has not defiled herself and is clean, then she shall be free and shall conceive children.

"This is the law in cases of jealousy, when a wife, though under her husband's authority, goes astray and defiles herself, or when the spirit of jealousy comes upon a man and he is jealous of his wife; then he shall set the woman before the LORD, and the priest shall execute upon her all this law. The man shall be free from iniquity, but the woman shall bear her iniquity."

The accusation is ultimately either proven or disproved by the fertility of the woman. Should she be guilty, her health and fertility leave her, her thigh shrivels and her body swells. In this case, we notice two of the three symptoms (withering and swelling) which Greeks associate with envy. This implies the woman's violation of her marital status is as much out of lust as it is covetousness, the latter being one aspect of the Hebraic concept of envy.

On the other hand, the bitter water will have no effect and the woman will be fertile if the accusation is proven false. The addition of fertility, rather than simply saying she will be unaffected, is important to understand here. We have already discussed the importance of fertility in a Semitic environment: if a family produces no offspring, the community is destabilized not only by having to care for the childless elderly, but contention will ensue over who will take possession of ancestral lands and possessions. These delicate balances are tipped by infertility, making this Law of Jealousy all the more powerful of a threat.

The second passage we are concerned with is in the prophesies of Ezekiel:

> RSV Ezekiel 8:3-12 He put forth the form of a hand, and took me by a lock of my head; and the Spirit lifted me up between earth and heaven, and brought me in visions of God to Jerusalem, to the entrance of the gateway of the inner court that faces north, where was the seat of the image of jealousy (*qanah*), which provokes to jealousy (*qanah*). And behold, the glory of the God of Israel was there, like the vision that I saw in the plain.
> Then he said to me, "Son of man, lift up your eyes now in the direction of the north." So I lifted up my eyes toward the north, and behold, north of the altar gate, in the entrance, was this image of jealousy (*qanah*). And he said to me, "Son of man, do you see what they are doing, the great abominations that the house of Israel are committing here, to drive me far from my sanctuary? But you will see still greater abominations."
> And he brought me to the door of the court; and when I looked, behold, there was a hole in the wall. Then said he to me, "Son of man, dig in the wall"; and when I dug in the wall, lo, there was a door. And he said to me, "Go in, and see the vile abominations that they are committing here."
> So I went in and saw; and there, portrayed upon the wall round about, were all kinds of creeping things, and loathsome beasts, and all the idols of the house of Israel. And before them stood seventy men of the elders of the house of Israel, with Jazaniah the son of Shaphan standing among them. Each had his censer in his hand, and the smoke of the cloud of incense went up.
> Then he said to me, "Son of man, have you seen what the elders of the house of Israel are doing in the dark, every man in his room of pictures? For they say, 'The LORD does not see us, the LORD has forsaken the land.'"
> (KJV Ezekiel 8:12 Then said he unto me, Son of man, hast thou seen what the ancients of the house of Israel do in the dark, every man in the chambers of his

imagery? for they say, The LORD seeth us not; the LORD hath forsaken the earth.)

This is a condemnation of envy, directly linking it to the idolatry of Israel. The connection between God seeing and their idolatry is also linked, with the Lord's anger over the fact that Israel thought He was blind (v. 12). In v. 6, Yahweh declared that He is far from the sanctuary, again a reference to Exodus, where God was met in the desert, not in the comfort of downtown Jerusalem.

But the Image of Jealousy also prevented Ezekiel from seeing, which is why he must be brought into the court through a hole in the wall. The blindness here was on the part of those who provoked to jealousy, the idolators.

Having reviewed the major prophetic voices of envy in the Old Testament, we shall move onto a more obscure but no less interesting symbol: the serpent. The serpent is the first creature to have interaction with Adam and Eve in the Garden, yet we have little direct information about him in the story. We must then conclude that he is a type of something. What is this type?

Isaiah 59:1-10 gives us a clear picture of the serpent concept:

> KJV Isaiah 59:1-10 Behold, the LORD'S hand is not shortened, that it cannot save; neither his ear heavy, that it cannot hear: But your iniquities have separated between you and your God, and your sins have hid his face from you, that he will not hear. For your hands are defiled with blood, and your fingers with iniquity; your lips have spoken lies, your tongue hath muttered perverseness. None calleth for justice, nor any pleadeth for truth: they trust in vanity, and speak lies; they conceive mischief, and bring forth iniquity.
>
> They hatch cockatrice (*aspidon* in Septuagint Greek, *tsepha* in Hebrew) eggs, and weave the spider's web: he that eateth of their eggs dieth, and that which is crushed breaketh out into a viper (*baskiliskos* in Septuagint Greek, *epheh* in Hebrew).
>
> Their webs shall not become garments, neither shall they cover themselves with their works: their works are works of iniquity, and the act of violence is in their hands. Their feet run to evil, and they make haste to shed innocent blood: their thoughts are thoughts of iniquity; wasting and destruction are in their paths.
>
> The way of peace they know not; and there is no judgment in their goings: they have made them crooked paths: whosoever goeth therein shall not know peace. Therefore is judgment far from us, neither doth justice overtake us: we wait for light, but behold obscurity; for brightness, but we walk in darkness.
>
> We grope for the wall like the blind, and we grope as if we had no eyes: we stumble at noonday as in the night; we are in desolate places as dead men.

Here we see the use of *aspis/tsephah* translated as 'cockatrice' in Old English while *basiliskos/epheh* is translated as 'viper.' A cockatrice is a legendary animal, also known as the basilisk (the second Greek term in the translation), which used its Evil Eye to kill its victims.[128] The translator of the KJV must have had some understanding of the Greek legends of the basilisk in order to insert the word.

There seems to be no consistent usage of the various words for 'serpent,' neither does there appear to be a consistent Septuagint translation from the Hebrew. The most common words for serpent are *aspis* or *ophis* in Septuagint Greek and *nachash* or *saraph* in Hebrew (c.f. Ge 3:1, Nu 21:8, Ps 58:1-5).

What we can see from the Old Testament (esp. Ge 3:1 & Ps 58) is that the serpent is associated with slanderous speech.[129] The *nachash* of Genesis 3 offers the lie which Eve and then Adam accept, thereby he defames Yahweh by bearing false witness against Him. This imagery appears again when Yahweh turns Moses' rod into a *nachash*, which swallows the serpents conjured by the Egyptian magicians. This first sign reveals the Egyptians' covetousness in refusing to give Israel back to God (Ex 7:9-10). When Israel grumbles against Yahweh and defames Him, He sends *nachashim saraphim* or 'fiery serpents' among them so that they might know their own slander (Nu 21:6-7). Moses is instructed to build a bronze *saraph*, or 'fiery serpent,' which will heal the people if they look to it in Verse 8. However, the next verse states that Moses made a brass *nachash*, not a *saraph*.

We believe that the reason for the change in language is that Yahweh looks at the *saraph* image as a messenger, performing the duty of an angel or *seraph*. The word *seraph* appears twice in Isaiah as angelic beings with human features. The connecting etymology surrounds the root of s-r-ph (in Semitic languages, there are word-families of related concepts based on two- or three-consonant patterns), which appears most frequently as 'burning' as with fire.

This is fascinating when we consider the earlier mirror theory of Siebers (that the Gorgoneion used by the Greeks to prevent the Evil Eye is a mirror to the envy of the viewer), through which we might interpret the bronze serpent as a mirror-revelation of Israel's defamation of Yahweh. By confronting their own poisonous mouths in the image of the serpent, they receive healing. The bronze serpent is a messenger revealing Israel's sin. For this reason, it is set up in the Temple as a sign of venomous mouths of the Israelites, who refused to believe in the Unlimited Good of Yahweh.

There is also a clear connection between murder and slander, with more references than we can dare catalog. The serpent's bite is associated with death in Near East culture. One point that should be emphasized is that venom and gall are considered the same both in Greek and Semitic thought.[130] Venom is spit forth, according to Greek philosophers such as Pliny, through the fangs but originating in the gall bladder.[131] In Mesopotamia, serpents were pictured as spitting venom, and this act was interpreted as symbolic of speaking.[132] Kings and potentates were capable of producing death by their decrees, something like Yahweh's own power in His Word. Gall or venom came from the mouths of powerful men, which they 'spit' upon the people and the land when they were challenged. This shows the connection between venom and the power of words.

Gall is associated with 'bitter' in uses other than venom, and we can see a parallel here to the 'bitter water' of the Rite of Jealousy in Numbers 5. Deuteronomy 32:32 uses both *marar* and *rosh* to express bitterness as poison and gall. In Psalm 58, *chemah* is used as venom, which can also be read as rage or indignation, but is clearly connected in this passage with slanderous lies.

This image of bitterness is at the heart of the Exodus commemoration, when the people partake of the bitter herbs when celebrating the Passover. This again alludes to the hardship one encounters before leaving the camp in Exodus to meet God, which reinforces the scapegoat imagery discussed earlier.

Archeological evidence suggests Semites (and Greeks) believed that only one animal that could overcome the serpent: the horse.[133] The long legs and hard hooves of the horse can trample down the serpent, thus victory is associated with trampling (*ramach*). This may hint of the imagery in Genesis 3:15, since the heel is the closest thing a human has to a hoof. This is probably also hinted at in the story of Jezebel's demise when she is cast from the tower and trampled by the horses (2Ki 9:33). The image of lifting up the heel against another to trample on them like a snake is a symbol of victory, while the inability to trample another is a sign that one cannot overcome one's enemies (c.f. Jb 18:9 & Si 12:17). This is seen in Jacob's firm grasp of Esau's heel, alluding to the envy between them and Esau's inability to overcome his brother (Ge 25:26).

The serpent (*nachash*) first appeared in Genesis as the tempter of Adam and Eve, and has been the topic of endless discussions in both the ancient and modern eras. Among the suggestions as to what the serpent was, many concepts have been put forth: a symbol of recurring youthfulness, earthly wisdom, chaos,[134] rebellion against God and even a cameo appearance by Satan himself. There are strong arguments to be made for all, and we believe the strength of the story lies in its purposeful ambiguity. The serpent evokes images of venomous whispers and lies, the *logos* of mankind in all its destructiveness.

Isaiah 27:1, Yahweh slays the leviathan, also referred to as a *nachash*, because of the bloodshed upon the earth mentioned in the previous verses. Leviathan becomes symbolic of the murderous sins of the inhabitants of the earth. The serpent is synonymous with murder, but in Genesis the *nachash* offers man the idolatry of being like God without God. Given our previous discussion of the Decalog, the connection should be quite clear. Idolatry, envy, slander and murder find their residence in the person of the serpent.

Conclusions

Our reader is now in a position to see the tip of the envy iceberg that floats within the Old Testament corpus. In this rushed treatment of the topic, we see how the Scriptures combine envy and greed into what might be likened to the 'grenvy' concept developed by psychologist Joseph Burke in his book *The Tyranny of Malice*.[135] Dr. Burke does not include stinginess in this idea, but we can see that modern psychology cannot utterly separate envy from other types of self-centered behavior. It is unlikely that many psychologists would find the Biblical concept presented here as completely objectionable if we merely replace 'idolatry' with 'selfishness' or 'narcissism.' The Bible suddenly takes on air of a textbook, teaching the reader about the inner workings of the human mind.

We have only one further question left to ponder, and that is how to explain the Old Testamental view of the Evil Eye to that of its Chaldean roots and later Jewish thought. How is it that Scriptural Judaism can appear so radically different from latter interpretations after the Babylonian Captivity? From the evidence already presented, we see a much 'higher' and less superstitious understanding of envy in the Old Testament, which appears totally lost on the rabbinic scholars who composed the later commentaries. We can only imagine the influence the Captivity had on Hebrew theology and self-awareness.

3

Christianity & the Evil Eye

St. Paul and the Epistles

The most significant eye event of the New Testament occurs with Christianity's greatest proponent, St. Paul. It is St. Paul, as the Apostle to the Gentiles, through which Christianity derived its exegesis of Scripture and thus was able to appeal to outside the Jewish community. His reading of Scripture made him the foremost of apostles and prophets, since he was the first to see Christ not in the flesh but in the Scripture itself. Thus, St. Paul's eyesight is a critical issue to Christianity: if his vision was somehow occluded or distorted, his reading of Scripture would be effected.

Let us consider Acts 9, when he received a vision of Christ on the road to Damascus, after which he could not see. After Ananias prayed for him, "something like scales fell from his eyes" and he could see (v. 18). Tarazi believes this incident explained Paul's reading of Scripture, specifically his reading of Isaiah (esp. chs. 41-42) in which the Gentiles come to Jerusalem to worship God.[136]

These 'scales' represent the blockages we have seen used as 'logs' and 'specks' in the Gospels, thus they were obstructions making his eye narrow towards the Gentiles. Paul realized that the Scripture dictated that he must have a larger or 'beautiful' eye (i.e., greater generosity and hospitality) towards the Gentiles and offer them salvation along with the Jews.

St. Paul realized that the Gentiles must be received into the Church as they are and not as Jews. The Judaizers were attempting to contradict Isaiah. If St. Paul was to account for the motivation of the 'narrow eyed' Judaizers, what natural accusation would he have? Of course, envy! St. Paul must then have used envy as a motif in explaining his reading of Scripture versus the narrow interpretation of the Judaizers. If the charge of envy were accepted against the Judaizers, St. Paul would be unchallenged in his exegesis: his opponents, because of their occluded vision, would be unable to read Scripture (i.e. their understanding was faulty). It should be obvious, both from common sense and our studies thus far of the Scripture, that envy impacts judgement.

While the word *vaskanía* only appears once in the Epistles, there are in fact more references to *phthonos* and *zelos* than in the Septuagint (minus the Apocryphal books). The theme of envy continues on from the Gospels into Acts:

> RSV Acts 5:17 But the high priest rose up and all who were with him, that is, the party of the Sadducees, and filled with jealousy (*zelou*)

> Acts 7:9 "And the patriarchs, jealous (*zelosantes*) of Joseph, sold him into Egypt; but God was with him,"

> Acts 13:45 But when the Jews saw the multitudes, they were filled with jealousy (*zelou*), and contradicted what was spoken by Paul, and reviled him.

> Acts 17:5 But the Jews were jealous (*zelosantes*), and taking some wicked fellows of the rabble, they gathered a crowd, set the city in an uproar, and attacked the house of Jason, seeking to bring them out to the people.

The second quote shows the author of Luke's Gospel had an awareness of the Old Testament theme of envy, expressed in his frequent use of *zelos* both in positive and negative contexts. Further, Acts' direct attribution of envy to the rabbis suggests that St. Paul was developing this concept in his preaching, and that the early Christian community was afflicted by the envy of the Jews. This explains St. Paul's often misunderstood quote:

> RSV Galatians 3:1 O foolish Galatians! Who has bewitched (*ebaskanen*) you, before whose eyes Jesus Christ was publicly portrayed as crucified?

In Galatians, St. Paul was defending his Gospel message from Judaizers.[137] Along with bringing their zeal for the Law, St. Paul implies that they had brought with them their envious (or 'narrow') eye, which put the Evil Eye (i.e., *vaskanía*) on the community. The Apostle then countered the Judaizers' lack of hospitality and Limited Good outlook by prying open the gates of heaven to the Gentiles (Ga 3:24-4:9). St. Paul's Greek readers understood this usage of *vaskanía* to mean magic and envy, witnessed by St. John Chrysostom's later use of this passage in his *Homily 2* (2:1). In this case, the manifestation of *vaskanía* appears not to be magic but rather the preaching of a different Gospel.

Envy is most often listed with other violations of the Decalog, usually as an accusation of utter depravity:

Romans 1:29-32 They were filled with all manner of wickedness, evil, covetousness, malice. Full of envy (*phthonou*), murder, strife, deceit, malignity, they
are gossips, slanderers, haters of God, insolent, haughty, boastful, inventors of
evil, disobedient to parents, foolish, faithless, heartless, ruthless. Though they
know God's decree that those who do such things deserve to die, they not only
do them but approve those who practice them.
See also Ro 13:13, Ga 5:19, 1 Ti 6:4, Tu 3:3 & 1 Pe 2:1

The most common sins listed with envy are slander and murder. There is also
the listing of *kakia*, which is usually translated as 'malice' (c.f. Ro 1:29, Tu 3:3 &
1 Pe 2:1). In the Septuagint, this word appeared as 'evil' or 'affliction' (c.f. Ge 6:5
& Ex 22:23). The association here is that to resent someone in this context is to
deny him or her salvation (a form of *mishpat*), which is evil. It is a failure to carry
out the *mishpat* or hospitality of the Old Testament by dividing the community
through sinful contention.

This contention, triggered by a Limited Good worldview, is often triggered by
love of honor as a manifestation of pride. The epistles linked envy to pride in several instances (c.f. Ga 5:26, Ph 1:15, & Ja 4:1-6).

The actual term *philotimia* (love of honor) is rarely used, and appears to have
degenerated from the classical Greek meaning to the very general term 'ambition'
(c.f. Ro 15:20, 2 Co 5:9 & 1 Th 4:11), but could also be a play on words that St.
Paul intended the reader to see his work as love of God's honor. The same change
has occurred with *zelos*, which can mean both 'jealousy' and 'zeal.'

St. Paul used *zelos* in Philippians 3:6 to describe his persecution of the Church
and adherence to the rabbinic interpretation of the Law. This usage seems contra-
dictory to his use of *zelos* in 2 Corinthians 7:7-9:2 and Romans 10:2-12:11.
However, the preaching out of *phthonos* in 1:15 parallels the *zelos* in 3:6. In effect,
St. Paul's reference to envious preaching earlier in the text helps the reader comprehend his own 'narrow-eyed' zeal in 3:6.

St. James' epistle has been the subject of an extensive study in regards to its
envy theme.[138] Luke Johnson compared James 3:13-4:10 to the apocryphal *Testament of the Twelve Patriarchs* and found eight similarities:

> ...(1) an explicit call to conversion; (2) the synonymous use of phthonos and
> zelos; (3) the attribution of envy to a pneuma [spirit] which is a deceiver; (4)
> the tendency of envy towards murder; (5) the role of envy in generating soci-
> etal unrest; (6) the turning from the evil spirit to God by prayer and mourn-
> ing; (7) the giving of grace by God to those who turn from envy (or Beliar)
> and turn to God; (8) the portrayal of envy's opposite as simplicity of soul and
> goodness of heart.[139]

This *pneuma* of envy is probably not a Hellenistic phenomenon, since it is mentioned in the curse of the bitter water in Numbers 5 we discussed earlier. This spirit seems to be a suspicion or a sudden temptation, which comes unexpectedly on a man. This can be interpreted in terms of the "accidental" Evil Eye which people, struck by such a spirit, will give another the Eye without malice aforethought.

Envy, both in the *Testament* and in *James*, are seen as antithetical to God and can thus be interpreted as a form or manifestation of idolatry. Obviously, the early Christian community recognized this concept in the Old Testament and in Christ's preaching.

As in the Gospels, the image of Moses' Bronze Serpent resurfaced in St. Paul's writings. In 1 Corinthians 10:1-10 the destruction by serpents was written of to warn future generations of the danger of idolatry and slander. St. Paul also uses the image of the slandering serpent as a metaphor for false teachers (c.f. Ro 3:1-19 & 2 Co 11:3).

So, we see that St. Paul used envy to explain the motivation of the Jews and the Judaizers who opposed his Gospel. He knew that forcing Gentiles to convert to Judaism was a formidable task, and that many would not receive the Gospel were they forced to change identities. Quite possibly he also realized that the primary motivation for Judaizing was a desire to limit entrance into the Kingdom of Heaven. Jews did not want to share the blessing of Abraham with outsiders. The easiest way to do this would be to bind a load too heavy for the convert to bear (Lk 11:46) or to make the convert go to such extremes that he would become a hyper-Jew (Mt 23:15). However, we can also see that St. Paul's primary concern was exegetical: the Judaizers were envious, thus narrow-eyed and unable to read Scripture as he could. After all, if envy did not matter, why did he go to such lengths to denounce it in his opponents?

St. Paul, in order to establish his reading of Scripture, had also to prove that his eye is 'good' and therefore unimpeded. He does this by portraying his enemies as envious, since this naturally implies the narrowness of their eyes. They cannot read Scripture properly if their eyes are blocked by 'specks,' 'logs,' and 'scales.' For this reason, Acts 9 is critical: when he is one of the Pharisees and encounters Christ, he becomes aware of the 'scales' in his eyes. When he repents, the 'scales' fall away. The natural assumption is that the Pharisees and Judaizers he left behind still have their 'scales,' and are thus unable to see and have right understanding as Paul does.

This makes St. Paul the sole authority on Scripture, as he is the only one with clear eyes. His enemies are 'blind guides' who are jealously guarding their honor as the sons of Abraham, not realizing that Abraham was blessed because he shared.

Envy thus become *the* impediment to the Gospel's spread. Not only does envy of God prevent one from accepting His gifts of forgiveness and healing, but it stops up the gate to the Kingdom. We see the power of the 'image of envy' in Ezekiel through the actions of the Judaizers, who battled to keep the Gentiles out of the plan of salvation.

If our assumptions are true to this point, we can now see how St. Paul's teachings influenced the composition of the Gospels. Since the authors used St. Paul's preaching and letters to inform their works, it is reasonable to assume that the theme of envy would arise in the Gospels. Thus, the Gospels would then be aligned to the Old Testament theme of envy and also lay the groundwork for St. Paul's charges. After all, if the Jews in the Gospels are shown to be envious, their inheritors (namely, the Judaizing Christians) would have the same charge laid against them as well.

The Gospel of Mark

Most scholarship seems to indicate that Mark is probably the oldest of the Gospels and was the pattern for Matthew and Luke.[140] In fact, Mark and Matthew use almost the same sentence for each of their single uses of the word 'envy':

> RSV Mark 15:10 For he [Pontius Pilate] perceived that it was out of envy (*phthonon*) that the chief priests had delivered him up.

> Matthew 27:18 For he knew that it was out of envy (*phthonon*) that they had delivered him up.

Roman Catholic scholars Anselm Hagedorn and Jerome Neyrey asked how it is that Pontius Pilate would have known this, and they then searched the Gospel of Mark for answers.[141] Using many of the same resources we have discussed already in this paper, Hagedorn and Neyrey analyzed the text and came to the conclusion that the Gospel centered on Christ's provocation of envy in the Jewish community.

The first mention of envious resentment is actually aimed at St. John the Forerunner (Mk 6:19) for his derision of Herodias' sin. St. John's piety gave his words a great deal of credibility, and his growing influence in the community became a threat to the Limited Honor of the Hellenistic Jews running Judea for the Romans. His denouncement of Herodias' illicit marriage was credible, yet it was probably seen by Herodias that St. John's fame was at her expense. Resentment and envy naturally followed.

In Mark's Gospel, Jesus became well known in Galilee (1:28), but soon could no longer teach in the towns because of the crowds drawn to Him (1:45). These crowds began coming from great distances based on His reputation (3:7-8, 6:32-34), and became unwieldy in size (3:20, 4:1 & 5:21). His reputation spread (5:20) and people marveled at His miracles and swamped Him with requests for healing (5:22-23, 27-28; 6:53-56; 7:31; 8:1; 8:22; 9:14ff; 10:1; 10:46-47). He became known to everyone (6:53-56, 7:24-25, 11:1-11).

People were astonished by His teachings, and for this reason the scribes and Pharisees sought to kill Him (11:18). Why were the people astonished? Obviously, because of His many miracles. But the rabbis heard and saw more than that. In 7:5-8, Jesus called the scribes and Pharisees 'hypocrites' by saying they are far from God even though they assumed to speak for Him. Since He claimed that they are keeping the laws of men and not God (Mk 7:6-8), Jesus indirectly accused them of idolatry. Their concern with external formulae, Jesus implies, leaves them open to far worse sins than mere legal torts:

> RSV Mark 7:18-23 And he said to them [His Disciples], "Then are you also without understanding [as the Pharisees]? Do you not see that whatever goes into a man from outside cannot defile him, since it enters, not his heart but his stomach, and so passes on?" (Thus he declared all foods clean.)
> And he said, "What comes out of a man is what defiles a man. For from within, out of the heart of man, come evil thoughts, fornication, theft, murder, adultery, coveting, wickedness, deceit, licentiousness, envy (*ophthalmos poneros* or Evil Eye), slander, pride, foolishness. All these evil things come from within, and they defile a man."

By accusing the Pharisees of these crimes, they are now Law-breakers and have an Evil Eye. From a common-sense perspective, Jesus argument is water-tight. Having silenced them, He has obviously deprived them of their honor by accusing them of having the Evil Eye and their refusal to repent and receive His correction.

Jesus' teachings were also astonishing because He came preaching the Unlimited Good of God. He initially called His Disciples away from their careers to follow Him without a clear explanation as to how they would care for themselves or their families (1:16-20). He extended precious and 'limited' salvation (in terms of the covenential Law and how the Pharisees understood it) to the sinful (2:17). He extended the limits of His family to include the crowds (3:31-35) and denied no one healing. His parables in Chapter Four depict the bountiful nature of the Kingdom of God despite what appeared to be insurmountable obstacles. Jesus sent His Disciples out to preach the Good News not depending on their own resources but on God's provision (6:7-13), then fed the multitude from five loaves of bread and two fishes (6:35-44, and again in 8:1-9 with seven loaves). When the discussion of provisions arose, Jesus chided the Disciples not for forgetfulness but their resolute lack of belief in the Unlimited Good (8:14-21). The miracles were so plentiful, in fact, that there is more than enough for the Jews and even the Greeks can share (7:25-30). His planning of the Last Supper was also a lesson in reliance upon God, in this case to provide a room for them (14:12-16).

Of course, with all this teaching under their belts, Christ then assigned them an even harder task: to give up everything for the Kingdom of God, resolutely trusting in God's provision through hardship and death (8:31-38). This was how He couched the teaching of the Resurrection that followed.

Jesus also warned His disciples not to become jealous when a man not numbered among them began casting out demons in Christ's name (9:38).[142] When the Zebedee brothers attempt to sway Jesus into making them greater than the other Apostles, the Disciples naturally became angry since their honor would be decreased (9:38-41). Jesus in both cases did not react, but rather calmly assures them that honor is not in limited supply. The exorcist was left to his business (therefore not decreasing the honor of the Apostles), and the Apostles were counseled to become servants and seek humility (eliminating honor as a measure of success). As we discussed earlier, these teachings are alien to both Greek and natural Semitic thought.

In 11:15, Jesus drove out the money-changers and animal-sellers from the Temple (also in Mt 21:12-13, Lk 19:45-46 & Jn 2:13-17). In doing so, He questioned the judgement of the priests who approved commerce in the Temple. The priests interpreted this in terms of Limited Good: Jesus was depriving the priests of honor by out-teaching and out-healing them, then embarrassing them over their faulty administration of the Temple.

This scene may also have further significance if we recall our earlier discussion of Ezekiel 8:3-12 and the Image of Jealousy in the gate of the Temple. In ancient times, commerce and trade were conducted in the gates of walled cities. This has to do with obvious traffic patterns and the desirability of a location in which everyone must pass through. Further, it was usually there that soldiers could be found guarding the gates, which is most comforting for merchants in a time before police patrol cars and radios. It is likely that the seats of the money-changers and animal merchants were in gates of the Temple as well.

Ezekiel encountered an 'image which provokes to jealousy' and its 'seat' in the gate of the Temple. If we consider the tables of the money-changers and their great business in the gate, it is not hard to see how commerce could easily have overtaken the worship of God. Both Matthew and Mark specify that the 'seats' of the animal-merchants were overturned, hearkening back to the 'seat' of envy in Ezekiel. Inside the Temple, Ezekiel saw the elders worshipping animals, a parallel image to the vain sacrifices of the Pharisees and the animal-merchants in the gate. It is entirely possible that this Gospel event is loosely patterned on the vision of Ezekiel, thus drawing the envy condemnations of the Old Testament into the life of Christ as presented in the Gospels.[143]

Returning to Jesus' interactions with the Pharisees, Hagedorn and Neyrey provide an analysis of Jesus' dialogs in terms of *chreia*. *Chreiai* are reminisces or accounts of questions and answers involving a teacher and either his pupils or opponents.[144] Questions were either posed to elicit an explanation of the instructor's beliefs, or to cause the instructor embarrassment. The *chreia* could be interpreted as challenges to the speaker's honor (*timé*), since a failure to provide a learned or witty answer would show his lack of learning. Therefore, these verbal battles were held in public to build esteem for the teacher in the eyes of the crowds.[145] If we recall our previous discussion of honor and envy, we know that honor is something ascribed to another by the community, and to lose honor meant that one also loses his place in the community and the possibility of material success. Further, those who posed the question to the teacher did so at significant risk: should the speaker trounce the questioner, the speaker's gain in honor would be at the expense of the questioner. To be deprived of one's honor is a classical set-up for envy.

In the case of Mark, Hagedorn and Neyrey identified numerous *chreiai*, all of which Jesus 'won' either by questioning or being questioned: 2:6-11; 2:16-17; 2:18-22; 2:24-28; 3:2-6; 3:22-30; 3:32-35; 6:2-5; 7:5-13; 8:11-13; 9:11-13; 10:2-9; 11:28-29; 12:13-17; 12:18-28 & 12:28-29.[146] The only place where Christ was denied honor was in Nazareth, as is recorded by all four Gospels. Hagedorn and Neyrey claim that Christ still 'won' the debate with the hometown crowd (despite their refusal to grant Him honor) simply by exposing their envious motives.[147] This is obvious, since Jesus' prophet status would have caused a loss of honor for others in the community, who jealously guarded their honor by refusing Christ His.

By the end of these challenges, the Pharisees had plenty of reason to envy Christ. Not only had he deprived them of their honor (invoking a natural jealousy reaction), but He had established Himself as superior to them. In terms of the Limited Good, the Pharisees had lost much, and their only option was to become envious.

Furthermore, Jesus was depicted as not seeking honor, which had to aggravate the Pharisees even further. A case for this is Mark 3:12, where he warns a man whom He heals not to divulge the Source of his healing. This may have been to show His humility, or it may have been yet another sign that Christ perceived the envy against Him and the danger this recently healed man faced.

This is expressed first through slander. In 3:22, the embarrassed Pharisees claim that Jesus cast out demons by the power of the devil. This slander is rather mild in comparison what was said of Him at the Cross, which we will explore next. One could also consider the accusations against Jesus and His Disciples in breaking the law to be slander once Jesus refutes them.

Slander and the Cross

During His trial, "many" bore false witness (Mk 14:56-59). But, the most symbolic and powerful act of slander occurred at the Cross. In 15:21-39, there are numerous events surrounding Jesus' crucifixion which hearken to the Old Testament. Twice (v. 23 and v. 36) Jesus was offered drink: first, wine mingled with myrrh; the second, vinegar (vinegar is also in Jn 19:29). Both are considered bitter, and Jesus refused to drink them. However, while we are often taught that the offering of vinegar and myrrh were either to numb the pain or to help Him die more speedily, this is contrary to the nature of the Crucifixion. To believe that these were mercies would contradict the utter abandonment He endured at the Cross; mercies shown by those who were unmerciful. Rather, we believe that these were in fact accusations against Christ as God, patterned on the accusation of infidelity in Nu 5:1-31.

Here, the Jews offer Christ a bitter drink, as a husband would offer an unfaithful wife the bitter water with a curse as in Numbers. It was a double accusation: if He was God, then they are accusing Him of being unfaithful. But, in doing so, they are reversing the Bridegroom-Bride relationship of Yahweh to Israel. Had Jesus drunk, He would have renounced His place as the Divine Bridegroom (c.f. Mk 2:19-20 & Mt 9:15). The envy of the Jews resulted in an attempt to deprive Christ of His identity as Faithful and Bridegroom.

Should this argument seem unclear, we ought to look at myrrh's underlying meaning. The Hebrew term m-r-r comes from Ugaritic, meaning gall or venom.[148] The same root appears in Hebrew, Syrian, Mandic and Aramaic, all of which translate it as 'gall' or 'venom.' In the Septuagint, the Hebrew word for 'poison' (*ro*), a derivative of *mrr*, is translated as 'gall' (*chole*),[149] which is the same root from which the English word 'myrrh' gets its origin.[150] While myrrh is pleasantly fragrant, it is also bitter to the point where it was used as a preservative when embalming corpses (thus, the 'myrrh-bearing women' of Orthodox Christian hymnology). This bitterness, associated with venom, hearkens back to our earlier discussion of venom and its association with slander. In essence, Christ was being offered the venom of accusation like the woman in Numbers (c.f. *m-r* in Nu 5:18, translated as 'bitter'). Although the Greek Gospel uses an etymologically different word, the understanding of bitterness is still there. This same incident arises in Matthew 27:34, this time the word 'gall' is used directly. This incident also accompanies the prophetic reference to His garments being distributed by lots, which we believe reveals the typology of the Old Testament at work with the drink as it is with the divided garments.

In route to the Cross, Christ was derided by being spit upon (Mt 26:67 & 27:30, Mk 14:65 & 15:19) which He predicted earlier (c.f. Is 50:6 to Mk 10:34 & Lk 18:32). While the spit of men is evil (like that of serpents which spit venom), Christ's own spittle is used to heal (Mk 7:33 & Jn 9:6). This shows the sweetness of Christ's words in contrast to the Jews' bitter and 'venomous' words.

John the Baptist called the Jews "vipers" for their appeal the Law which they did not keep (Mt 3:7 & Lk 3:7), as he must warn them to carry out hospitality to the poor as demanded by *mishpat*. Jesus takes the same appeal but adds to it:

> RSV Matthew 12:31-37 Therefore I tell you, every sin and blasphemy will be forgiven men, but the blasphemy against the Spirit will not be forgiven. And whoever says a word against the Son of man will be forgiven; but whoever speaks against the Holy Spirit will not be forgiven, either in this age or in the age to come.
> "Either make the tree good, and its fruit good; or make the tree bad, and its fruit bad; for the tree is known by its fruit. You brood of vipers! how can you speak good, when you are evil? For out of the abundance of the heart the mouth speaks. The good man out of his good treasure brings forth good, and the evil man out of his evil treasure brings forth evil. I tell you, on the day of judgment men will render account for every careless word they utter; for by your words you will be justified, and by your words you will be condemned."

Here, we see a link between the serpent imagery and slander, but also the connection between words and the heart. The "blasphemy" here is definitely slander, defined as slander against Christ and the Holy Spirit. Later in Matthew, Jesus again called the Pharisees 'vipers' at the end of a long string of accusations of hypocrisy (Mt 23:33), which hinted that the Pharisees' sins are epitomized as slander. If we recall the incident of the Bronze Serpent, it is Israel's 'grumbling' (i.e., slandering Yahweh by accusing them of leading Him to the desert to die) that brings death. To blaspheme is to slander, and to slander is to bring death for which there is no forgiveness.

We can also see signs of projection in the accusation of unfaithfulness against God. Throughout the Old Testament, Yahweh accuses Israel of being an unfaithful bride. At the Cross, Israel's convicted conscience is projected onto Jesus. He becomes the unfaithful one, a symbolic scapegoat for the sins of a straying Israel. We often assume that it was the Father who placed the sin of the world upon Christ, but it would seem that Christ's persecutors were also projecting their sins upon Christ as well. We will return to this later.

Christ's crucifixion with two robbers (Mt 27:38, Mk 15:29, Lk 23:35 & Jn 19:18) is also an important aspect of this projection of envy. The first hint of envy in Christ's execution narrative is Barabbas, who is released by Pilot rather than Jesus at the request of the Jews. Barabbas is described as a *listis*, which can be translated as 'robber' or 'rebel' implying the use of force in his stealing.[151] Another term used for one who steals, but by stealth, is *kleptis* (c.f. Mt 24:43 & Lk 12:29). Within Judaism, a robber received less punishment than a thief (Dt 24:7), since the latter committed his crime when no one else but God was watching, thus blatantly disregarding His sovereignty and ability to see (c.f. Is 29:15, Ps 94:7, Ez 9:9).[152] Barabbas' release implies that Christ's crime was worse than simply taking another's things, but that he lacked the honor to confront those from whom He was "stealing" and disregarded Yahweh's omniscience.

Our discussion of envy in Semitic thought, when applied here, made the robbers envious men for certain, and the equivalent to thieves in John's Gospel (10:8-10 & 12:6). Christ equates robbers with thieves, since both wait in ambush (i.e., hiding) to attack (Lk 10:30-37). The robbers' company at the Cross thus reveals the projection of envy placed upon Him by the community.

The equation of thieves and robbers to envy is why Christ appeals to the image of robbers in describing the Pharisees (Jn 10:8-10). They disregard Yahweh's commandments with their 'narrow' eyes, forgetting that He sees all and carrying out sinful commerce in the Temple gates as if waiting in ambush (Mt 21:13, Mk 11:17 & Lk 19:46). Thus the Pharisees prey on the unsuspecting people coming along a "known path" (i.e., the road to Yahweh's house, laden with offerings for Him that the robbers end up stealing).

This scapegoat image is mirrored in the Gospels since Christ was also led out of the city as the scapegoat was, with Simon the Cyrene leading the way (Mt 27:32, Mk 15:21 & Lk 23:26). Simon is described in Matthew and Luke as coming out of the country, so he is not part of the slandering rabbinic community. The fact that a man other than the rabbis or Romans led Christ on His Exodus out of the city lends itself to the concept of a holy man leading the scapegoat out of the Temple into the wilderness. The fact that the Crucifixion is referred to as an "exodus" during the Transfiguration should make this point abundantly clear (c.f. *exodon* in Lk 9:31). This exodus imagery is only strengthened by the Lord's first 'exodus,' when His family fled to Egypt during Herod's slaughter of the innocents, mirroring the Twelve Tribe's journey into and out of Egypt. The ministry of Christ began and ended with Exodus, in response to the envy of men. This is why His family did not return to Bethlehem: they more than likely would have faced the jealousy of families still grieving their losses.

Whereas the Old Testament scapegoat was not directly sacrificed, Christ as Scapegoat was. Christ is the final Scapegoat, since He is the only one whom we see actually sacrificed. From this point forward, there is nowhere else men may lay their sins. The two goats can be interpreted as foreshadowing the Old and New Covenants, one being sacrificed at the Temple altar while the second is led into the desert baring the burdens of men. The scapegoat was a symbol of Christ, who bore the burdens and destroyed them in His bloodshed.

The Gospel of John picks up on the scapegoating theme by noting the parallel between Moses' Bronze Serpent as a symbol of the people's slander and Christ's Cross. Both images bring "light" (i.e., the ability to see), recalling how *saraph* can mean 'messenger,' 'fiery' and 'serpent' as the passages below reveal:

> RSV John 3:14-21 And as Moses lifted up the serpent in the wilderness, so must the Son of man be lifted up, that whoever believes in him may have eternal life.
> For God so loved the world that he gave his only Son, that whoever believes in him should not perish but have eternal life. For God sent the Son into the world, not to condemn the world, but that the world might be saved through him. He who believes in him is not condemned; he who does not believe is condemned already, because he has not believed in the name of the only Son of God. And this is the judgment, that the light has come into the world, and men loved darkness rather than light, because their deeds were evil. For every one who does evil hates the light, and does not come to the light, lest his deeds

should be exposed. But he who does what is true comes to the light, that it may be clearly seen that his deeds have been wrought in God.

People are saved by seeing the fruit of their sin, which is bloodshed. They must see the murder their wicked envy results in, thus making *the Cross a messenger of the Law*. By seeing the bloodshed of their deeds, the people can have eternal life because they are able to repent as they were exhorted to in the beginning of the Gospel (Mt 3:2, Mk 1:15 & Lk 13:3).

The bloodshed of Christ is also the fulfillment of the Law as He promised in Mt 5:17. His blood completes the cycle of idolatry-envy-murder while at the same time preventing us from murdering so long as we accept His blood as the fruit of our sins. There are many instances in the epistles in which 'love' is spoken of as the fulfillment of the Law (c.f. Rm 8:4 &13:8-10, Ga 6:2 & Jm 2:8). The authors look to this extreme act of self-sacrificing as the model for love.

So, we are now left with the Bronze Serpent replaced by the Cross as a symbol of mankind's idolatrous enviousness and God's love for us. After all, why did Yahweh provide the Bronze Serpent to save Israel? Was it not out of the same love that He sent His only-begotten Son? Christ's proclamation in Matthew 5:17-18 that He has come to fulfill the Law also signals that Christ's crucifixion proves the idolatry of men. He fulfils the Law by provoking the Jews to envy and murder as the cycle of the Decalog outlines, and revealing that this very enviousness is turned towards God. Ultimately, the Jews' disbelief and idolatry result in the murder of the God they claimed to worship, a God they envy because of His perfection.

All men are guilty of the murder of God, therefore, if they are envious. The Gospel reveals a level of bloodlust that will stop at nothing until the death of the other (which is symbolic of the death of the self) is achieved. Judas' suicide out of desperation reveals the lack of satisfaction in enviousness, making the Cross both a warning and a way out. We are warned that our selfishness will result in another's death, and yet we are offered the opportunity to see Christ's death as the bloodshed resulting from our particular sins. By looking to the Cross and being illumined by its fiery message, we can repent.

Gospel of Matthew

In the Book of Matthew, our first evidence of an envy theme is in the Massacre of the Innocents in 2:1-18. Herod, upon hearing that the "King of the Jews" (i.e., a rival) had been born, plotted to have the infant Christ killed. When his plan was foiled, he ordered all the male children in the region slain. Jesus was a threat to the Jewish establishment's honor from his birth.

Jesus was tempted by the devil to reveal His power for His own gain (Mt 4:1-11), and Satan's final offer was to entice Jesus to commit an act of idolatry. This is rather odd when one remembers that the devil is speaking to God. However, idolatry is a central theme of Matthew's Gospel, as we will see later. For the time being, we can think of it in terms the devil's envy: he desires to be God and thus deprive Him of His identity. It is, in short, the desire to destroy God. If He had bowed down, as improbable as it was, He would have contradicted everything the Old Testament said of God.

From 4:23 to the end of Chapter 7, Jesus taught what we would consider the "Unlimited Good" of God (c.f. 6:25-34) as we saw developed in Mark. He preached that affliction and trouble will be reconciled by the Lord. In the end, the Gospel noted that He taught "as one who had authority, and not as the scribes" (7:29) which clearly is a setup for the scribes to become envious of Him.

Many of the same things we have seen in Mark also come up in Matthew, so we won't go into detail here. Jesus was also slandered (c.f. Mt 10:25) as in Mark, and engaged in the same teachings and debates. A key difference in the *chreiai* of Matthew is the use of the term 'hypocrites' (*hypokritai*), which occurs 12 times. The word originates from the Greek term for 'actor.'[153] Why did Jesus use this term for the Pharisees? Clearly, they were the most concerned with fulfilling the Law, and are probably the most moral of the Jewish population. Yet, they emphasized the outward acts of religion (6:2-15) and in fact were not interested in the Kingdom of Heaven except to keep others out (23:13).

This last verse is important, and brings us back to the earlier discussion of Ezekiel's prophesy. Shutting up the Kingdom of Heaven could be a reference to the "image of jealousy" in Ezekiel, since the Temple was once the means to the Kingdom of God. The selling of animals and the changing of money had so clogged the gates that they had rivaled the activity inside the Temple itself. The Pharisees created an idol out of the trading necessary to properly execute the Law as they saw it (e.g. animals and proper currency).

Christ's indictment of "hypocrisy" for the idolatrous religious activity around the Temple lays the groundwork for the Jews' envy and murder of Christ. Jesus' actions in Matthew (less apparent in Mark) are a purposeful provocation. Quite literally, Jesus is drawing out their idolatrous behavior so that the Pharisees will become envious and murder Him.

Christ's Teachings on the Eye

Jesus also teaches His disciples the Biblical understanding of vision. Rather than using the Greek notion of the eye emitting light into the world, Jesus explains to His Disciples how the eye's light affects what comes into the eye, making the Biblical 'light of the eyes' an inward rather than outward light:

> RSV Matthew 6:22-23 "The eye is the lamp of the body. So, if your eye is sound, your whole body will be full of light; but if your eye is not sound, your whole body will be full of darkness. If then the light in you is darkness, how great is the darkness!"

> Luke 11: 33-36 "No one after lighting a lamp puts it in a cellar or under a bushel, but on a stand, that those who enter may see the light. Your eye is the lamp of your body; when your eye is sound, your whole body is full of light; but when it is not sound, your body is full of darkness. Therefore be careful lest the light in you be darkness. If then your whole body is full of light, having no part dark, it will be wholly bright, as when a lamp with its rays gives you light."

This is a complete renunciation of Greek vision theories and visual rays, reversing the emanation inwardly rather than externally. The image is illuminated *by the eye* as it enters and passes into the viewer, affecting his entire being. This is again a reference to the limbic/neocortical functions of the brain as discussed in *The Eye of Mishpat and Hospitality* in Chapter Two.

Jesus warns His followers to be careful *how* they see. They are not supposed to hide their eyes (Lk 11:33), but make certain their eyes are not 'dark' (i.e., they have an ungracious attitude towards what they see). This is connected with a 'narrow eye' which would not be as bright as a 'beautiful eye,' as we recall our previous discussion of this concept in the Old Testament. There is also the idea that it is better to pluck out an evil eye than to allow it to darken the whole being and cause one to fall into Hell (Mk 9:47 & Mt 18:9).

A reference to the Old Testament concept of the "narrow eye" can be seen in Jesus' teaching regarding the camel and the needle (Mt 19:24, Mk 10:25 & Lk 18:25). The rich man[154] could be seen as one with a "narrow eye," since he has stored up for himself many goods and not shared with the poor. The needle has a narrow eye, so much so that a camel cannot pass through it. The "narrow eye" of the rich man does not allow good to pass through in either direction, it sees no good nor does it permit its goods to be shared. The eye of the needle is thus compared to the rich man's eye, not the gate to the Kingdom of Heaven. The gate is open to all those who act out of mercy and righteousness, the opposite of those who act out of greed and envy, storing up for themselves wealth.

This is why each instance in Matthew, Mark and Luke is followed by an exclamation from the disciples that they have abandoned their possessions and followed Him. In leaving what they have, others have benefited from their wealth and they have proved their reliance upon God's Unlimited Good. They are defending their own "good eyes" in the face of Christ's teaching, which explains their defensive remarks.

There may also be an argument for the splinter and log story in Matthew 7:3-12 and Luke 6:41-45 being a referenced to the "narrow eye." Both sayings involving logs in the eyes are followed by references to generosity, both of God (Mt 7:7, 11-12) and loving men (Mt 7:9:10 & Lk 6:43-45). The log in the eye is directly linked to the generosity of the heart in Luke 6:45. It is also worth noting that generosity and the "good eye" (e.g. without a log) is linked with the Word (Mt 7:12b & Lk 6:45b). The log therefore is a narrowing of the eye, some kind of blockage that prevents one from acting with the hospitality required by the Law. Jesus condemns those who judge their brother's *mishpat* when they themselves have a narrow eye.

The "speck" or "log" is a character defect or a failure to see things clearly because of something in the way one sees. It is wrong, according to the parable, to criticize and offer remedies when one cannot act mercifully towards others. Christ's mission was to open the eyes of the Jews who refused to see with a "good eye" but instead used a "narrow eye" in limiting forgiveness and salvation to themselves (c.f. Mt 23 & 15:14).

Direct references to *ophthalmos poneros* are few in the Gospel, but are certainly worthy of mention.

> RSV Matthew 6:23 but if your eye (*ophthalmos*) is not sound (*poneros*), your whole body will be full of darkness. If then the light in you is darkness, how great is the darkness!

> KJV Matthew 20:15 Is it not lawful for me to do what I will with mine own? Is thine eye evil (*ophthalmos sou poneros*), because I am good?
> *See also Mark 7:20-22*

We see nothing surprising here in these three quotes. The Evil Eye and the heart are definitely linked here in terms of ethical disposition. There is no hint of Hellenistic "visual rays," nor is there any notion of Evil Eye as a substantive defilement.

The first quote sits in the middle of the extensive Matthean quote of Jesus' ethical teachings, beginning with the Sermon on the Mount. In the Sermon, Jesus states that the pure in heart will see God (Mt 5:8). We see here that the inward condition of the man effects his ability to see. The theme of blindness in the Gospels is extensive, and we do not have time to explore it in great detail. What we can deduce is that a narrow-eyed man (who is therefore hardened in his heart towards others) is unable to give what the Law requires in terms of generosity, and therefore it unable to see God.

So connected are the eye and the heart that to look and see sin is to commit fornication. By this we can see that the eye assigns a sinful value to the image, which is not the image itself but rather the value assigned to it. While we could say more about this, we will stay with the theme of the Evil Eye for the time being.

Stepping back to the Sermon, the Beatitudes attack typical Greek and Semitic thought in regard to social status. Poverty and suffering were assumed to make people envious of those who were prosperous. The Beatitudes reverse this dialectic, making those who are suffering more blessed by granting them eternal gifts. Scholars have noted that in the Beatitudes Jesus compares the evil eye (Mt 6:23 has (*ophthalmos sou poneros*, while Lk 11:34 has *poneros*) with the *haplous* or healthy eye.[155] Professor John Elliott notes that the meaning of *haplous* is both 'healthy' and 'single,' and bears with it the connotation of moral integrity.[156] This term is the subject of an essay in the apocryphal *Testament of the Twelve Patriarchs*, and was described in the text as an attribute of Joseph in juxtaposition to his Evil Eyed brothers. Morality was seen as simplicity of intentions, while the envious had complex reasons and motivations for their actions. We may also conclude that an Evil Eye is not 'single' because it contains obstructions that add to it.

Envious Choking in the Gospel

In pre-Christian Greek iconography, artists sought to create a language of physical gestures to suggest different emotions. Relying solely on facial expressions would have relegated artistic efforts to the few remarkable talents, and so a much more vivid and less detailed system of visual cues were necessary. Greek artisans commonly settled on three body poses suggesting the subject was suffering from envy: choking (either by hanging or hands at one's own throat), withering or swelling.[157] These poses are all borrowed from Greek literature that used the same descriptions to illuminate characters suffering from envy in their writings.

Choking provokes an interesting picture, since it implies than nothing can come out or go in. The envious cannot consume what they desire, nor can they expel their feelings of inadequacy.

> RSV 4 Esdras 16:77 Woe to those who are choked by their sins and overwhelmed by their iniquities, as a field is choked with underbrush and its path overwhelmed with thorns, so that no one can pass through!

This is the same choking which overcomes the word in Jesus' parable of the sower (Mt 13:22, Mk 4:19, Lk 8:14). It is the desire for wealth overcoming the desire for the Word of God which is indicative of an envious man by Biblical standards, since he is unwilling to give God His due. This is the case with Judas, who greedily accepted money to betray Christ. This appears in all the Gospels except John, who instead recorded Judas' indignation when Mary anoints Jesus with a flask of expensive nard (12:1-6).

The words *zelos* and *phthonos* are not used in reference to Judas, but there are hints that he is envious. In Matthew 27:3-5, Judas gave back the money of his betrayal of Christ, then hanged himself. This shows several symptoms of envy as we have previously discussed: Judas "choked" on the money, unable to have it; while at the same time he had no peace despite betraying Jesus as he planned. Judas' envy was not assuaged, and only with Jesus' murder could he see his hopeless state.

A curious example of this concept of the envious choking on money arose during the Robber Synod of Ephesus in 449.[158] Bishop Sophronius of Tella was deposed for practicing magic, one incident involving the *tyromanteia* or 'cheese-sandwich test.' After ordering several suspected thieves to swear their innocence on the Gospel, the bishop performed a pagan ritual and forced the suspects to eat a cheese sandwich under his watchful gaze. The man who choked on the sandwich was assumed to be the culprit, since the magic rite would reveal the envious thief through an obvious sign. Since this first operation failed, the bishop resorted to *phialomanteia* or divination using oil and water to detect the envious culprit. This practice continues to this day for detecting the Evil Eye.[159] Of course, just as at that time, such wizardry is not to be expected from a Bishop!

Hanging is also indicative of envy, being that it is a type of choking.[160] Greek art occasionally depicted the envious as hanging themselves. So, Judas' hanging in Matthew 27:5 is evidence of his enviousness. The only other account of Judas' demise is Acts 16:20, where Judas "bursts" just as Greek art would have depicted him with the assumption that he was envious. Clearly, Luke's colorful description was most likely to help readers better understand Judas' motives, which were not so clear in the other Synoptics. St. John's accusation that Judas was a thief (Jn 12:6) made his suicide a fulfillment of the Law (Dt 24:7) since his enviousness made him a murderer according to the Old Testament (Ex 22:2, Jb 24:14 & Pr 29:24).

This strangulation motif explains the use of the Cross in His execution. We need not go into great detail other than to say that the cross is an instrument of asphyxiation. The Jews attempted to choke Jesus to death on the Cross, which would then prove in a symbolic way that He was envious (remember our earlier discussion of projected envy). Strangulation was also considered an accursed death in the Scriptures (c.f. Jb 7:15, Tb 3:8 & Nh 2:11-13), hanging being the foremost (Dt 21:23, To 3:10 & 2 Sa 17). The Book of Acts mentions the prohibition on the eating of strangled meats in 5:20, 5:29 and 21:25 based on Le 13-15. This has to do with the blood remaining in the meat, because the blood has life in it. This has an interesting implication when we consider the Eucharist and Christ's commandment to eat His flesh (c.f. Mt 26:26, Mk 14:22 & Lk 22:19). Christ's broken body contains lifeblood, so much so that when He was stabbed with a spear blood and water immediately came out (c.f. Jn 19:34). This surplus of fluids is an anti-image of envy: Christ has plentiful fluids, rather than withering away from envy.

Malice and Forgiveness

When the Pharisees accused Christ of exorcising demons in the name of Beelzebub (Mt 12:24 & Lk 11:15), the Lord gives a multi-part answer worth analyzing. The Gospel of Matthew recorded this, which is duplicated in Luke's narrative:

> RSV Matthew 12: 25-37 Knowing their thoughts, he said to them, "Every kingdom divided against itself is laid waste, and no city or house divided against itself will stand; and if Satan casts out Satan, he is divided against himself; how then will his kingdom stand? And if I cast out demons by Beelzebul, by whom do your sons cast them out? Therefore they shall be your judges.
> "But if it is by the Spirit of God that I cast out demons, then the kingdom of God has come upon you. Or how can one enter a strong man's house and plunder his goods, unless he first binds the strong man? Then indeed he may plunder his house.
> He who is not with me is against me, and he who does not gather with me scatters. Therefore I tell you, every sin and blasphemy will be forgiven men, but the blasphemy against the Spirit will not be forgiven. And whoever says a

word against the Son of man will be forgiven; but whoever speaks against the Holy Spirit will not be forgiven, either in this age or in the age to come.

"Either make the tree good, and its fruit good; or make the tree bad, and its fruit bad; for the tree is known by its fruit. You brood of vipers! how can you speak good, when you are evil? For out of the abundance of the heart the mouth speaks. The good man out of his good treasure brings forth good, and the evil man out of his evil treasure brings forth evil. I tell you, on the day of judgment men will render account for every careless word they utter; for by your words you will be justified, and by your words you will be condemned."

By testifying to His own power in verses 25-29 (judging by the number of demoniacs He heals, the rabbis were not successful exorcists), Christ establishes that His worth ought to elicit gratitude. He had brought the Kingdom of God in their midst, witnessed by the collapse of demonic opposition. In verses 31-32, He allows forgiveness for men who speak ill of Him, but not those who slander the Holy Spirit. The final lines condemn the poisonous slander of the Pharisees, coming from their evil 'treasure.'

The key to this passage is in verse 30, where He claims all who are not for Him are against Him. Those who are against Him are thus defined as those who slander Him in response to His goodness. The Pharisees are ungrateful for what He has given Israel, and so they are against the Christ. He does not give them individually a choice to accept the gift He has given to all men, so their only option is to glorify God for the miracles. Instead, they slander Him.

Christ's miracles fall upon those who are grateful. The crowds of people who flock to Him, and we see many acts of gratitude for the forgiveness and healing He brings. He does not forgive the Pharisees. Neither do the Pharisees thank God for the exorcisms they have seen, but instead they act enviously towards Him. Since the Gospel ties forgiveness to healing, we can assume that the message here is that envious malice *against God* is the only impediment to receiving God's forgiveness. After all, the tax collectors and 'sinners' are involved in all sorts of envious behavior towards one another, but they all receive Christ without envy and malice.

Malice and envy towards God are therefore the definition of damnation. Hell is not a punishment meted out by God as some would have it, but a refusal of a pardon granted all mankind. It is impossible to receive good from a person one envies, and so it is that one cannot be saved if one resents God. This is the message of the Prodigal Son in Luke 15:11-32 when the elder brother refused to enter the house when his brother returned. He resented his father's forgiveness and kindness, and so he would not enter the feast. Malice and forgiveness are antithetical.

Conclusions

The New Testament provides a colorful exposition of envy and its practical manifestations. Complex theories are ignored as we see greed and envy swell up to the point where man seeks to kill the Immortal and burn down the Created Order upon himself. We see envy and greed acted upon, inducing guilt. In the struggle to liberate the conscience, the self-idolater transfers his sins to another so that he might free himself and survive his own rage at his injustice. He is then free to immolate the one onto whom he had transferred his sins.[161] Sadly, this purification is an illusion, as Judas discovered. All of his anger at Christ was really intended for himself, and the Crucifixion proved it.

Had Judas or the Pharisees admitted their guilt, they would have found hope in the Cross. But, since their envy was aimed at the only one who could save them, they shut themselves out of the Kingdom.

4

the Post-Apostolic Age & the Evil Eye

Developments in the Envy Theme in Church Writings

Our previous exploration of the Old and New Testaments was confined to looking for specific terminology and obvious themes connected to envy and the Evil Eye. We did not discuss Satan in great detail, nor the mechanics of the Fall of mankind in the Garden of Eden. This chapter will deal with these topics in terms of how they were understood by early theologians.

It might also seem to the reader that what has been presented here thus far is a new revelation of some 'hidden' information within Scripture. Instead, we believe that it has only been in recent times that envy has been sidelined as a major theological concept. Our evidence that envy was once a major theological concept is a long list of Holy Fathers who mention the centrality of envy to the fallen condition of man. The following section will present a few references in roughly historical order, so that the reader can see the continuity of this concept through time. The prominence of envy in Church writings disappeared with time not out of any dramatic shift in theology, but its glaring obviousness. There was no need to discuss what was plainly apparent to everyone. In addition, the great eloquence of early writings on the topic made restatement a redundancy.

For us to list all of the condemnations and observances of envy to be found in the Fathers, this book would be impossibly long to read. What we will explore is the concept, already developing in the Fathers we have covered, of envy as a form of Primordial Sin.

While the West has the notion of Original Sin, which makes all men guilty of the sin of Adam passed down through the act of conception, the Orthodox Church believes that all men are born enslaved to an ancestral curse of sin. We are not guilty of Adam's sin, but are instead given the propensity to sin as a result of the ancient Fall. If envy is the sin of Adam and Eve in the Garden (something we did not discuss in the Old Testament section because the Hebrew word *qanah* does not appear in reference to the incident), then our whole understanding of the Cross and Redemption is changed. Christ's death was to save us from the same envy that murdered Him. Envy and death are then the same thing.

Nearing the first century AD, a revolt in the Church of Corinth triggered a lengthy epistle by a Roman bishop named Clement.[162] Clement's primary concern was for the good order of the Church, and so he sought to educate the Corinthians as to what ailed their community. His letter immediately launches into the topic of envy, which he blames for sewing discord among the brethren.

Clement complimented the Corinthians for their reputation of hospitality and humility, thus setting the standard to which his letter would hold them to in his epistle. In the letter, he describes the rebellion of younger Christians against the elders as being incited by envy. After citing many cases of envy in the Old Testament, Clement blames the martyrdom of St. Paul and others on the envy. He sees envy as the source of all destruction.

In calling the young Corinthians to repentance, he invokes the memories of Abraham and Rehab, which were examples of generosity. He calls them to humility and to not follow the envious words which entice them to sedition. For Clement, peace and envy are as opposite as oil and water. Thus, he urges them to silence in the face of the slanderous words of the envious.

Justin Martyr condemns Jewish ritual ablutions in comparison to Christian baptism when he says:

> "For what is the use of that baptism which cleanses the flesh and body alone? Baptize the soul from wrath and from covetousness, from envy, and from hatred; and, lo! the body is pure."[163]

He states elsewhere that it is envy that makes men turn to idols,[164] and so he keeps with the Scriptural notion that idols are nothing but symbols of men's selfish desires (c.f. Isaiah). Justin assumes that the serpent is the devil, even going so far as to say that the name 'Satan' is a derivative of "fallen serpent" in Hebrew.[165]

Theophilus of Antioch was the first early Christian scholar to quote Wisdom 2:24 to explain death.[166] He also saw envy as the motivation for the devil's use of the serpent in the Garden (he does not identify the serpent as the devil himself), and then later:

When, then, Satan saw Adam and his wife not only still living, but also begetting children—being carried away with spite because he had not succeeded in putting them to death,—when he saw that Abel was well-pleasing to God, he wrought upon the heart of his brother called Cain, and caused him to kill his brother Abel. And thus did death get a beginning in this world, to find its way into every race of man, even to this day.[167]

St. Irenaeus of Lyons also noted the enviousness of the Jews[168] and the devil[169] in the Gospels. He also posited that Yahweh rejected Cain's sacrifice because his heart was divided with malice and envy.[170] For St. Irenaeus, apostasy was motivated by envy:

Just as if any one, being an apostate, and seizing in a hostile manner another man's territory, should harass the inhabitants of it, in order that he might claim for himself the glory of a king among those ignorant of his apostasy and robbery; so likewise also the devil, being one among those angels who are placed over the spirit of the air, as the Apostle Paul has declared in his Epistle to the Ephesians, becoming envious of man, was rendered an apostate from the divine law: for envy is a thing foreign to God. And as his apostasy was exposed by man, and man became the [means of] searching out his thoughts, he has set himself to this with greater and greater determination, in opposition to man, envying his life, and wishing to involve him in his own apostate power. The Word of God, however, the Maker of all things, conquering him by means of human nature, and showing him to be an apostate, has, on the contrary, put him under the power of man. For He says, "Behold, I confer upon you the power of treading upon serpents and scorpions, and upon all the power of the enemy," in order that, as he obtained dominion over man by apostasy, so again his apostasy might be deprived of power by means of man turning back again to God.[171]

He also mentioned that the apostasy of the devil occurred after the creation of man, since the devil's envy was of God first, then later men.[172] Primarily, the devil's envy seemed to Irenaeus to be rooted in the worship of God by men, since the brunt of the devil's envy is directed towards us. This makes the devil the first idolater. We should emphasize that there appears to be no clear consensus among the Fathers on this matter. What can be certain is that none of the Fathers would deny that the devil was envious. Other saints had also made forceful arguments that Satan's primary sin, shared by men, is that of pride.

The sin of pride is certainly strong, and we believe it has great merit. Pride can best be associated with idolatry, since a proud man makes an idol out of himself. Such an argument fits with Scripture. But pride assumes one already possesses honor that must be defended. Envy assumes awareness of one's lack of honor, much as Satan and man would have felt in comparison to God. Pride may be conjured to cover over one's inadequacies, but this makes it *envious pride*, pride at another's expense as it were.

In St. Athanasius' *On the Incarnation*, he quoted Wisdom 2:4 in describing how envy caused man to die and set in motion all other sins (5:2-3).

> For because of the Word dwelling with them, even their natural corruption did not come near them, as Wisdom also says: "God made man for incorruption, and as an image of His own eternity; but by envy of the devil death came into the world." But when this was come to pass, men began to die, while corruption thence-forward prevailed against them, gaining even more than its natural power over the whole race, inasmuch as it had, owing to the transgression of the commandment, the threat of the Deity as a further advantage against them. For even in their misdeeds men had not stopped short at any set limits; but gradually pressing forward, have passed on beyond all measure: having to begin with been inventors of wickedness and called down upon themselves death and corruption; while later on, having turned aside to wrong and exceeding all lawlessness, and stopping at no one evil but devising all manner of new evils in succession, they have become insatiable in sinning.[173]

St. Athanasius also stated that what is good cannot envy at all, making envy and goodness antithetical. He believed that God is good and therefore kind, something that the envious cannot be.[174] He blamed the envy of the Jews not only for the death of Christ but their own destruction as a nation.[175]

In the *Life of Moses,* St. Gregory of Nyssa used some of the same word pictures to describe envy that we have seen in Greek thought (i.e. 'bitter poison' as in slander and emaciation). He called envy,

> The passion which causes evil, the father of death, the first entrance for sin, the root of wickedness, the birth of sorrow, the mother of misfortune, the basis of disobedience, the beginning of shame. Envy banished us from Paradise, having become the serpent to oppose Eve. Envy walled us off from the tree of life, divested us of holy garments, and in shame led us away clothed with fig leaves. Envy armed Cain contrary to nature and instituted the death which is vindicated seven times. Envy made Joseph a slave. Envy is the death-dealing sting, the hidden weapon, the sickness of nature, the bitter poison, the self-willed emaciation, the bitter dart, the nail of the soul, the fire in the heart, the flame burning on the inside...[176]

Here, the saint made the remarkable suggestion that envy was the serpent in the Garden of Eden. Our previously quoted Fathers all connected envy to the devil, but here St. Gregory took the image usually said to be the devil himself and replaced Satan with envy. Envy then became the seducer, and Eve was overcome by it. Thus, the devil's enviousness of man became his entire being, and the only thing he could offer man is to share in his being. By being envious, man shared in what it is to be the devil.

St. Gregory repeated this same identification of the devil as envy itself when he wrote:

> Indeed the great Job will not be jealous if he who imitated him be decked out with like testimonials of praise. But Envy, that has an eye for all things fair, cast a bitter glance upon our blessedness; and one who stalks up and down the world also stalked in our midst, and broadly stamped the foot-mark of afflic-tion on our happy state.[177]

From the Book of Job, we know that the devil stated that he walks up and down the earth when asked by God to give account of himself. And here, it is envy that now trods the earth looking to afflict men. Earlier in the same oration, he alluded to Envy (through the agency of death) stripping men of their fine gar-ments and leaving them with sackcloth. This allusion to Adam and Eve's predica-ment is hard to miss.

It would appear from the samples taken that at least some of the Fathers equated the Primordial Sin of Adam and Eve as one of envy. The reader might find it obvious that the devil was motivated by envy to seduce Adam and Eve, but how is it that Adam and Eve themselves were envious? Let's explore this a moment: the word envy was not used in Scripture to describe Adam and Eve, but their actions betrayed them: 1) Eve believed the slander of the devil over the goodness of God as she had known it, 2) the couple stole the fruit, 3) they desired to supplant God's supremacy with their own and so steal His identity as God, 4) they sought to hide their inadequacy once it had been discovered and 5) Adam slandered Eve by blaming her for their joint actions. It is not improbable that the Fathers saw Adam and Eve in this light. Certainly, the Fathers saw envy in humanity after the expulsion.

Treatises on Envy

Stepping back a century from St. Gregory, St. Cyprian (circa 250 AD) devoted an entire treatise to our topic, appropriately named *On Jealousy and Envy*.[178] The fact that he separated the two concepts reveals his Hellenistic education on the matter. His outlook, however, is solidly Christian, given the fact that he used them throughout the treatise as an inseparable pair. The saint warned his reader against laughing off one's own envy, seeing it as a constant source of danger to one's life. Cyprian also equated envy with self-destruction as the envious struggle against their brethren with homicidal intentions.

The saint also rejected the concept of visual rays in favor of the Biblical concept of passive vision. Through temptations (first through the eyes, leading to unchastity), the devil fires darts at the unwary believer, one of which is enviousness. What is ironic in Cyprian's treatise is that the devil himself envied man for being made in the image of God, thus killing himself while also seeking to kill humans. Having reduced himself with his envy, he struggles to bring men down with him. Thus, envy is both the devil's destruction and his weapon. Quoting Wisdom 2:24, Cyprian faults the devil's envy for introducing death into the world.

Cyprian then goes on to list the many envy tales of Scripture: Abel and Cain, Jacob and Esau, David and Saul, and finally Christ and the Jews. This sin is a "gnawing worm of the soul" and "rust of the heart" from which countless other sins develop. It not only seems boundless in history, but also in its hunger for destruction. The saint even prefers sword wounds to envy!

The central wound of the envious are their blindness to God's goodness and mercy, which makes them dangerous within the flock of Christ. Turning to St. Paul in 1 Corinthians 13, Cyprian says the envious are discerned by their lack of *agape* or love. This love brings about the peace that marks believers as vessels of the Holy Spirit. In rejecting rancor and malice, one can receive the riches of God. And, it is with God looking down upon the reader that St. Cyprian charges his audience to look to Him and receive His goodness

One of the most developed early treatises on the Evil Eye was composed by St. Basil the Great (circa 370 AD) in his Homily 11 *Concerning Envy*.[179] Like St. Cyprian and other Fathers before him, St. Basil also equated envy with the devil. He stated that there is no worse vice than envy, and then lamented the suffering of the envious. To St. Basil, the envious suffers more than anyone else, tortured by the good of others and ashamed of his condition. His language is medicinal:

the envious need healing, which they will find in the Scriptures. This is something we can all agree with considering the earlier chapters of this work.

St. Basil condemned the kind words of the envious after the fall of their victims, and went on to call them "hypocrites," just as the Lord condemned the Pharisees. This behavior is likened to a fountain of death or a reef to passing ships. The envious try to cover their tracks with false praise, something sociologists have noticed in studying envy in human relationships.[180]

As he continued, the bishop returned to the same Old Testament figures as St. Cyprian, finally arriving at the crucifixion of Christ. Here, be blamed the Jews for envying Christ for His miracle of *providing salvation* for the needy (i.e. unlimited salvation). The Jews were envious because Christ shared the divine abundance with men, and the Jews could not, so their malice grew.

St. Basil recommended that the faithful not have friendships with envious people, quoting Solomon from Ecclesiastes 4:4. His argument was that the envious only have affect on those whom they are intimate with. In rejecting the Greek notion of visual rays, the saint wrote:

> As arrows shot with great force come back on an archer when they strike a hard and unyielding surface, so also do the movements of envy strike the envious person himself and they harm the object of his spite not at all. Who, by his feelings of annoyance, ever caused his neighbor's goods to be diminished? But the envious person pines away with grief…the devils, who are enemies of all that is good, use for their own ends such free acts as they find congenial for their wishes. In this way, they make the eyes of the envious persons serviceable to their own purposes.

He derided the belief in the Evil Eye as a special power of the eye as "popular fancies and old wives' gossip." Instead, he saw the Evil Eye as slander against anything good. He described the withered appearance of the envious, sounding a great deal like the withering associated with envy in Greek thought. What makes envy all the more preposterous is that the things it yearns for often have no "intrinsic good" in them. Were they gathered for their own sake, these things would actually be evil. This reveals the depravity of the envious: they desire good things in an evil way, thus making good things evil.

St. Basil states that those who are generous with their wealth are indeed righteous and deserve praise. If we resent the deserved praise of another, we are envious and thus deny that it is God who provides all. St. Basil is a champion for the unlimited good of God and the universal ownership of the Almighty rather than men.

Church historian Matthew Dickie has noted a strong parallel between St. Basil's treatise and the writings of Plutarch.[181] What is recognized is that the saint rejected out-of-hand the philosopher's conclusions regarding vision, though the historian was disappointed that St. Basil did not also reject the idea that Christians were subject to demonic attack instigated by the envious intentions of others. To this day, no Orthodox Christian would take such a stand: all Christians are subject to assaults from the devil, but strength in belief and reliance on God govern the success of the attack. An elementary reading of *Philokalia* would set the matter straight.

St. John Chrysostom also mentioned the Evil Eye directly in his *Commentary on Galatians* (ch. 3:1) when he said:

> Observe too how soon he stays his arm; for he adds not, Who has seduced you? Who has perverted you? who has been sophistical with you? but, "Who hath cast an envious eye on you?" thus tempering his reprimand with somewhat of praise. For it implies that their previous course had excited jealousy, and that the present occurrence arose from the malignity of a demon, whose breath had blasted their prosperous estate. And when you hear of jealousy in this place, and in the Gospel, of an evil eye, which means the same, you must not suppose that the glance of the eye has any natural power to injure those who look upon it. For the eye, that is, the organ itself, cannot be evil; but Christ in that place means jealousy by the term. To behold, simply, is the function of the eye, but to behold in an evil manner belongs to a mind depraved within. As through this sense the knowledge of visible objects enters the soul, and as jealousy is for the most part generated by wealth, and wealth and sovereignty and pomp are perceived by the eye, therefore he calls the eye evil; not as beholding merely, but as beholding enviously from some moral depravity. Therefore by the words, "Who hath looked enviously on you," he implies that the persons in question acted, not from concern, not to supply defects, but to mutilate what existed. For envy, far from supplying what is wanting, subtracts from what is complete, and vitiates the whole. And he speaks thus, not as if envy had any power of itself, but meaning, that the teachers of these doctrines did so from envious motives.[182]

We see here the same notions of passive vision and the active role of the devil in the Evil Eye phenomenon. People act because of their Evil Eye rather than the Evil Eye being an action in itself.

Prayers for the Evil Eye

Prayer has often been a way men have struggled against perceived assaults of the Evil Eye. One of the oldest and most vivid intercessions dates back to the Sumerians, approximately 5,000 years ago:

> The eye is a single ox, the eye is a single sheep,
> The eye is numerous men, the mouth of numerous men,
> The eye is evil, the most evil thing.
> Asarluhi saw this, he went to his father Enki in the temple and he spoke thus to him:
> "My father, the eye is a single ox, the eye is a single sheep!"
> A second time he spoke:
> "What shall I do I do not know, what can cure him?"
> Enki answered his son Asarluhi: "My son, what do you not know? What can I add?
> "Asarluhi, what do you not know? What can I add?
> "What I know, you also know. Go my son, black wool and white wool, bind around his head."
> The evil eye of the evil-doing man. May it be slaughtered like an ox!
> It is an incantation against the Evil Eye.[183]

This prayer mentions one of the talismans used to deal with the Evil Eye, but sadly depicts the powerlessness of the deities to protect people from this dark force. Charms and threats seem to be the best defenses men are offered. We may consider this less of a prayer than a magical incantation, but there is an appeal to a god for help. But, an incantation is different from a prayer: with a prayer the deity is powerful, but an incantation is considered a power unto itself. This is exemplified by Enki's admonition to Asarluhi to use wool rather than ask for divine intervention. Enki is just as weak as his son in the face of the Evil Eye.

Judaism picked up Evil Eye beliefs after the Babylonian Captivity. Since the Evil Eye was deeply entrenched in Jewish magical beliefs (we are now speaking of the power of the eye rather than moral disposition), we do not have a corpus of Jewish prayers but rather Scriptural recitations and incantations as defense. Amulets and talismans were often employed to ward off the eye, most of which were written forms of these incantations and recitations. Images such as the eye and the phallus were not used, revealing the Jewish preference for Divine texts over *mana*-baring symbols.

A prayer implies a total reliance on God's immediate intervention for an otherwise defenseless supplicant. Because the Jewish magical tradition gave special powers to the rabbis, there seemed to be a greater emphasis on the personal power of the rabbi. Studying Torah and leading a moral life gave him powers, which he could then use against the forces of evil. His power originates from God through Scripture, and so Scripture was the weapon. Lengthy prayers about the Evil Eye do not appear, but there are several priestly blessings or *berakhot* that Jews uttered when they felt under assault from the Evil Eye.[184]

Christianity assumed no such power. While Jewish magic tradition preserved the idea of human dependence on Yahweh and his angels through the employment of Scripture and holy names, Christianity assumed that only a personal interaction with God was both permissible and effective. For this reason we have a stunning collection of prayers for blessing almost anything and making just about any request imaginable.

There are examples of ancient Christian-like magic incantations. It is unclear whether such formulas were used by pagans employing Christian names and themes. We can assume that at least some Christians fell into or were not entirely released from superstition, but these objects and practices were hardly condoned by the Church. Here is an example of an amulet incantation text that used Christian, Jewish and Egyptian themes in combating the Evil Eye:

> CH M G Hor Hor Phor Phor, Yao Sabaoth Adonai, Eloe, Salaman, Tarchei, I bind you, artemisian scorpion, 315 times. Preserve this house with its occupants from all evil, from all bewitchment of spirits of the air and the human evil eye and terrible pain and sting of scorpion and snake, through the name of the highest god, Naias Meli, 7 times, XUROURO AAAAAA BAIN-CHOOOCH MARIIIIIIL ENAG KORE. Be on guard, O lord, son of David according to the flesh, the one born of the holy virgin Mary, O holy one, highest god, from the holy spirit. Glory to you, O heavenly king, Amen. AW AW IXThUS[185]

Even to this day a prayer for the Evil Eye can be found in the most recent editions of the Greek *Evchologion*. We are not aware of any previous studies of this prayer, and we cannot comment reliably on its origin. It is highly likely that this prayer is a fairly late addition, as it is absent from Goar's *Evchologion* and the Slavonic *Trebnik* presently in use in the Russian Orthodox Church. While this prayer was not included in the Arabic *Evchologion* translated by St. Raphael Hawaweeny, the Arabic version of this prayer is presently used by Antiochian clergy in the Middle East. Various parishes of the Greek Archdiocese of North America distribute translations of this prayer to the faithful, often in competition with lay "healers" and home remedies for the Evil Eye.

Below is a translation by Fr. Evagoras Constantinides in his *Mikron Evchologion,*[186] which I reworked slightly for better clarity:

> Let us pray to the Lord...Lord, have mercy.
> 1. O Lord our God, the King of the ages, almighty and all-powerful, who createth and changeth all things by Thy will alone; 2. who changed the flames of the Babylonian furnace into the dew after being heated seven times more than usual and preserved in safety Thy three holy youths; 3. the physician and healer of our souls; the security of those who hope in Thee; 4. we pray Thee and beseech Thee: Remove, drive away and banish every diabolical activity (*diabolikin energeian*), every Satanic attack (*satanikin ephodon*) and every plot, evil curiosity and injury, and the evil eye (*ophthalmon baskanian*) of mischievous and wicked men, from Thy servant (N.); 5. and whether it was brought about by beauty, or bravery, or happiness, or jealousy and envy (*phthonou*), or evil eye (*baskanias*), 6. do Thou Thyself, O Lord who loveth mankind, stretch out Thy mighty Hand and Thy powerful and lofty Arm, and look down on this Thy creature and watch over him (her), 7. and send him (her) an angel of peace, a mighty guardian of soul and body, who will rebuke and banish from him (her) every wicked intention, every spell and evil eye (*baskanian*) of the envious and envious men; 8. so that, guarded by Thee, Thy supplicant may sing to Thee with thanksgiving: "The Lord is my helper, and I shall not be afraid; what can men do to me?" [He 13:6] And again: "I shall fear no evil for Thou art with me." [Ps 23:4]
> 9. For thou art our God, my strength, the powerful ruler, the prince of peace, the Father of the ages to come. 10. Yea, Lord our God, spare Thy creature and Thy servant (N.) from every injury and insult brought about by the evil eye, and keep him (her) safe above every ill. 11. Through the intercessions of our most blessed and glorious Lady Theotokos and ever-Virgin Mary, of the radiant Archangels and of all Thy saints. Amen.

First, we should note that the Evil Eye appears elsewhere in prayers of the Church. In the "Prayer for the Woman After Childbirth," God is asked to protect the mother from "sickness and infirmity, jealous and envy, and from the Evil Eye" in the Slavonic version.[187] The Antiochian version is considerably reduced through editing, yet continues to mention the "jealous eye."[188] This prayer is commonly used in most parishes and its authenticity has not been questioned. We must then conclude that there is an accepted concept of the Evil Eye in the Church.

Second, we ought to look at the vocabulary used in the prayer. *Vaskanía* is a word with two meanings as we already know. It means both envy and Evil Eye, as opposed to *phthonos* which can be translated either as 'jealousy' or 'envy' (the latter is preferred)[189] as we have discussed earlier. In short, there are no surprises in this prayer

So, *vaskanía* has both a moral (envy) and magical (Evil Eye) meaning. It is often associated with emanations, but the Evil Eye can also be conjured. Therefore, it is tied to the world of the demonic, since spiritual beings are often called upon in magic and also the very existence of demonic possession points out the envy of demons towards those who live in bodies.

So, now we return to the prayer to see if this does indeed measure up to the standards set by the Scriptures as expounded by the Holy Fathers that we have discussed in the previous section. We will comment on each line of the prayer separately.

Line 1—a normal opening to a prayer, calling to remembrance the invincibility and universal jurisdiction of God over all things.

Line 2—this line, invoking the image of the Three Youths in the furnace, is clearly in keeping with St. Basil's understanding of the Evil Eye: their steadfastness in faith resulted in God's rescue.

Line 3—this recalls Christ's self-description as the healer, which therefore acknowledges that the person being prayed for is indeed sick. The symptoms and illness are not specified.

Line 4—this list of afflictions begins with the activity of demons, and categorizes them with the Evil Eye and the possibility of witchcraft (i.e., the actions of 'mischievous men'). The fact that they are lumped together implies a single origin with various manifestations. The fact that the Evil Eye of men is the only human attribute while all the rest are demonic actions therefore makes the human activity of lesser concern.

While there is mention of 'injury,' it should be pointed out that this is an ambiguous term. Injury could mean either physical and spiritual, and since the source implied is the devil, we can deduce that it probably means some type of spiritual injury. This would explain why 'evil curiosity' precedes it, which is not a physical affliction.

Line 5—this is a rather puzzling list that is supposed to represent the reasons why one might be afflicted. This is obvious for the first three attributes (beauty, bravery and happiness), but the last two (envy and the Evil Eye) appear to be means of affliction. We believe that the reason for lumping envy and the Evil Eye into the category of attributes that trigger the affliction could be understood in several ways. It may be that the reason the person is complaining of the Evil Eye is that the person being prayed for is suffering from envy himself. His complaint may be a projection of his envy onto the other who has "struck" him. Therefore, the reason that he is ill is his own envy.

Another explanation may be that simply believing that one is vulnerable to the Evil Eye is in fact a reason for being struck by it. This is a list of liabilities: person assets worthy of envy and the general presence of envy in society. By being concerned about these things, the person has invited affliction upon himself. In psychological terms, this line functions to assuage guilt for having more than one's share of good. It makes the victim 'envy-worthy,' a comforting place to be in when one is suffering. The Evil Eye functions as a way for one to acknowledge blessings and not feel guilty about it.

Line 6—this is a common reference to the strength of God to protect the afflicted person from all threats. The image of the Hand of God was also commonly used by Jews (and later Muslims as the "Hand of Fatima") as an amulet against the Evil Eye.

Line 7—our liturgical services frequently ask God to provide a Guardian Angel, usually at the Dismissal. Here, the same angel is requested to protect the person being prayed for from: **a.** every wicked intention (this does not specify human or demonic), **b.** every spell (i.e., the action of and/or cooperation with demonic forces), **c.** evil eye of the envious (again, the 'envious' are not specified as men or demons) and **d.** envious men. The last is very specific about men being envious. Why the repetition? We believe that the first occurrence of 'envious' (**c.**) is speaking of the envious demons and not of men, thus confining human agency to the last position on the list (**d.**). If this is the case, we might be able to transfer our understanding of the list in Line 4 and apply it here to Line 7. Lines 4 & 7 are parallel in structure, especially if one notices the use of 'and' in the sentence, thus making the last attribute of each sentence the only reference to human activity in regards to envy.

Such an understanding would reflect the Bible and the teachings of the Holy Fathers. Since both Lines 4 & 7 specify the Evil Eye of men without specifying how the eye manifests itself, it allows for interpretation as physical and/or spiritual assault with the former being the Scriptural and Patristic understanding. What is important is the preeminence of demonic activity over human agency, and the vagueness with which the human agency is described.

Line 8—here we have several Scriptural quotes that remind the person being prayed for that, as a Christian, God is always with him and protecting him. This protection is from both men and from demons, and thus the subject of the prayer is being instructed not to *fear*. This emphasis on fear seems to be aimed at preventing people from obsessing over whether they have been struck with the Evil Eye. These two passages clearly leave no room for worry over the Evil Eye.

Line 9—this is again a remembrance of God's protection for the one being prayed for. There is a single shift to the singular ('my strength') which makes the line appear to be another exhortation to confidence in God's protection (notice also the reference to the 'prince of peace,' as if to further call the subject to calmness out of worry).

Line 10—this line appears to reinforce the earlier exhortations to confidence in Christ's protection and to stop the concern over the Evil Eye. That it mentions 'every ill' seems to be a diminution of the power of the Evil Eye, lumping the person's affliction with every other simple malady. This could be a way for the prayer to be binding if indeed there is no Evil Eye or demonic activity involved.

Also, the Evil Eye is mentioned here as the source of 'insult' and 'injury.' While the latter might be understood to happen through magic, insult is strictly a physical act (i.e., the spoken word). If we hold to the Biblical teaching of the Evil Eye (i.e., moral disposition), then these two attributes are restatements of the 'slander' and 'bloodshed' which the Bible associates with the actions of the envious (c.f. Is 59:1-10 & Ps 58:1-5).

This prayer then is a protection against the physical violence of men, rather than magical attacks. This narrows what is being prayed for at the ends of Lines 4 and 7, making the 'wicked/envious men' capable not of an Evil Eye in terms of special powers, but rather a threat in terms of slander and bloodshed. Therefore, all references to men's 'Evil Eyes' are nothing other than their ability to physically strike out. This physical threat is probably why 'insult' and 'injury' are mentioned with 'every [physical] ill.'

Line 11—this is a normal ending to a prayer.

One of the most striking aspects of this prayer is that there is no direct call to healing. The person who is the subject is assumed to have a physical malady, and yet the prayer does not even mention the reason why the person might think he has been struck by the Evil Eye. The only mention of illness is in Line 10, and it is speaking of the future.

We might conclude that an affliction caused by the Evil Eye is not an illness, and that despite the physical manifestation there is nothing wrong with the body. With this logic, we can say that the symptoms are immaterial to the cause.

Or, we might also take this a step further and suggest that the prayer itself is to lift demonic delusion from the subject because he has been deceived into believing that he has been injured by another's eye. However, the prayer is subtle enough that it will not immediately offend someone who firmly believes in the human Evil Eye. This would allow the priest to read this prayer over the person and pray that God will eventually reveal that one need only worry about the demonic Evil Eye rather than special powers neighbor's eye.

Clearly, the prayer acknowledges that the demonic can and does harm people, yet this prayer discounts the aspect of human agency. Humans are a threat through their direct actions rather than magical conjuring. It also affirms that there is nothing demonic can do that Christ cannot stop.

This also clarifies the meaning of the "Prayer for a Woman After Childbirth." Instead of a magical force of the eye, the prayer is clearly an invocation against the demonic powers, as seen in the fuller context of the second prayer of the three read over the woman:

> O Master, Lord our God, Who wast born of our Most-holy Soveriegn Lady, the Theotokos and Ever-Virgin Mary; Who, as an infant, didst lay in a manger and wast carried as a little child: Do Thou Thyself have mercy on this, Thy handmaid who has given birth today to this child. Forgive her all her transgressions, both voluntary and involuntary, and protect her from every oppression of the devil. Preserve the infant who has been born of her from every spell, from every cruel thing, from every storm of adversity, and from evil spirits, whether by day or by night. Keep this woman under Thy mighty hand and grant her speedy recovery, and purify her from uncleanness, and heal her sufferings. Grant health and strength of soul and body, and compass her round about with bright and radiant angels; and preserve her from every approach of invisible spirits; yea, O Lord, from sickness and infirmity, from jealousy and envy, and from the evil eye. And have mercy on her and on the infant, according to Thy great mercy, and cleanse her from bodily uncleanness and various afflictions of her womb. And by Thy quick mercy lead her to recovery in her humbled body. Vouchsafe the infant who has been born of her may worship in the earthly temple which Thou hast prepared for the glorification of Thy holy Name. For unto Thee are due all glory, honor and worship: to the Father, and to the Son, and to the Holy Spirit, now and ever, and unto the ages of ages. Amen.[190]

Again, the entire context of this prayer has to do with demonic assault rather that the eyes of men. Even spells can be considered demonic activity rather than the power of humans, since demons are relied upon to carry them out. Human agents are not mentioned. Also, there is no particular concern for the infant, though in superstition it is the child that is most likely to be afflicted with the Evil Eye.

Returning to our original prayer, it should be clear that is does not exactly follow the pattern of a healing prayer. Not only does it not focus on a call to healing, but it fails to mention the sinfulness of the person being prayed for, which most healing prayers contain. It does not involve an anointing or a sprinkling, nor does it fit the typical format of a sacramental prayer (e.g., anointing of the sick) with psalm readings, a Great Ektenia or a Dismissal. It fits into the category of minor supplications (e.g., Prayer for a Home Troubled by Evil Spirits, Prayer When in Fear of Earthquakes, etc.) and is not necessarily a priestly prayer (no mention of vestments or any liturgical act), so it could be read by a deacon or a layman if need be.

When compared to exorcism prayers, the Prayer for the Evil Eye is rather mild. There is no recounting of Christ's victory over the devil, nor is there any address aimed at Satan. Instead, there is a great deal of comforting language: the focus is on protection from evil (lines 1-3 & 6-11) rather than any deep concern over the subject's present situation other than the petition in Line 4 for immediate removal of demonic oppression. The prayer seems mostly intended to comfort the sufferer to trust God and not to worry about attacks from the Evil Eye.

We can also see that there is no notice made of *phylactos* or charms against the Evil Eye which are popularly used today. We will discuss the various amulets used throughout history to prevent the Evil Eye later in this chapter. While there is a prayer for the blessing of a neck cross or an icon (a medallion would likely fit into the latter category), none exists for the blue beads or eye pendants often employed against the Evil Eye. We can see they are not part of the Christian Tradition.

So, we believe it is entirely reasonable to assume that this prayer is Scriptural and keeps within the teachings of the Orthodox Church. It does not appear to expound Hellenistic beliefs regarding emanations from the eyes, but instead attributes affliction either to self-delusion or assault of the demonic.

Fear and Superstition

As we approach the end of this journey through the Evil Eye, it is appropriate that we return to where we began: fear and superstition. The Scriptural concept of Unlimited Good is counter-intuitive to our observations of nature. Environmentalism and free-market economics are both based on the concept of limited supply, and to say otherwise in any social gathering is likely to get one dismissed as a crank or a heretic.

Dualism is also much easier to believe in when we see the advances and longevity of evil people, along with the constant repetition of the darker aspects of human history. Evil and Good seem to have an even match, and the only reason many believe Good must triumph at some later point is merely to stave off utter desperation.

With this in mind, we will briefly explore the area of Evil Eye magic as it pertains to Christianity and our modern circumstances. As with all previous sections of this book, we continue to alert the reader that this is a summary of a great deal of material.[191]

The last section began with an Evil Eye incantation from the Sumerian period. There appear to be two primary ways that Sumerians dealt with the Evil Eye: prevention by a talisman or amulet, or curing after an attack through herbal medicine and ritual purification.[192] The wool threads, seeds and stones were often employed to prevent the Evil Eye from striking someone. Those fallen ill with the Evil Eye were treated with rituals including incantations, anointings with special oils and even cleansing with bread. Sumerian and Akkadian records do not make an effort to explain how the Evil Eye functions, and so we must look to later records for more in-depth discussions on the topic.

Greek discussions of the Evil Eye were informed by observances in two arenas: nature and the physiology of vision. The Greeks thought, for example, that certain animals killed with an Evil Eye (i.e. the basilisk), while other animals employed talismans against the Evil Eye (i.e. wood-pigeons surrounded their nests with bay tree shoots to protect their young from the Evil Eye).[193] We will not rehash earlier discussions of Greek theories of vision, having said enough already on physiology.

Greek magic employed many of the same principles as the Sumerians.[194] Talismans and amulets were carried by most people to fend off envious glances, either by distracting the envious person (and thereby the glance), reminding the viewer of the ugliness of envy, or providing a positive mana to counteract a negative one. In the first case, a figurine with odd features or a bead with bright colors acts to distract the first glance of the envious (particularly if the enviousness is a momentary impulse or inadvertent), and so the brunt of their evil emanations hit the charm. The second amulet might be a Gorgoneion or an image of an eye being assaulted by animals, which triggers a momentary pause in the envious person's assault. We may liken this to the 'eye spots' of animals, but with an intellectual bend: the amulet reminds us to look inward to see if we are envious. The final category, into which we find such amulets as *phalloi* that act as symbols of life or water.

Greek magic also focused on divination. Omens and fortune-telling were an important part of Greek life.[195] These were condemned in the Old Testament, and so we can assume that the Greeks followed even more ancient magic customs.

Although the Law condemns magic and witchcraft, the long exposure of the Hebrews to magic practitioners eventually rubbed off. Unable to resist temptation, Jews began to dabble in magic, using the Scripture both as a defense of their divinations and a tool.[196] Gideon's fleece, rather than an exceptional incident, became an excuse to dabble in the occult. Some rabbis were uncomfortable with such practices while others readily bought into magic. Their insurance policy against falling into evil was an emphasis on the invocations of holy names (i.e. God and His angels, 70 names in all) and the use of Scripture.[197] So long as men claimed dependence on God for magic, the practice was accepted. As for Jewish Evil Eye beliefs, they were entirely Hellenized and completely undifferentiated from Greek beliefs other than a dim understanding of demonic forces at work in the background.[198]

This reliance on written defenses changed the art of amulet- and talisman-making. Judaism's reliance on names and texts rather than images made magic much more of a written art. Instead of a phallus to counteract the Evil Eye, a Jew might wear a silver tube containing a scroll of Scripture.[199] The *hamsa*, or 'hand' amulet, represented the hand of God (a popular motif in Jewish iconography) was a popular symbol used to bear texts stamped into its surface.

Hand gestures have long held power in the ancient mind. Greek and Roman art often communicated emotions through the positioning of hands like a form of silent grammar. The outstretched and rigid fingers of the *hamsa*, tightly held together, to this day symbolizes "stop!" This sign, however, seems to go back much further than late Judaism. The Etruscans and Phoenicians used a similar gesture in their amulets.[200] To the Egyptians, the hand was a sign of divinity when depicted as radiating from the solar disc. Thus, the hand is a sign of force, divine or otherwise. Christian iconography to this day uses the gesture of the extended hand as a symbol of the power of God and as a blessing. So popular is this symbol that even rather iconoclastic Muslims have no qualms with wearing a *hamsa*, so long as it is identified as the Hand of Fatima (the daughter of Mohammed, who often helped him during bouts with the Evil Eye).

Late Judaism became increasingly magical with the development of Kabbalah and other esoteric practices. Jewish magic also infected their health concerns, so much so that talismans equaled herbal remedies and became part of normal medical treatment.[201] This is most likely the source for later Christian condemnations of visiting Jewish doctors (c.f. Canon 11 of the Council in Trullo), since many of their 'prescriptions' had less to do with physiology than with spiritism. As late as

1235, a trial murder trial in Fulda, Germany, concluded with the confession by a group of Jews that they had killed the five children to procure their blood for healing magic.[202]

Amulet inscriptions fell into six general categories (since they were hand-made, one amulet could have components of several categories): general benedictions, health, Evil Eye, miscarriage, fertility (business, agricultural and personal) and protection of mother and child in childbed.[203] These categories summarized the daily concerns of not only Jews but of nearly every person of that time. The latter categories were concerned with Lilith, an apocryphal character thought to be Adam's first wife, who deserted him.[204] She was blamed for infertility and child-murdering (we note the rather high infant mortality rate of that era) out of her envy of the fertility she was denied for abandoning her husband. Her Greek counterpart is Gylou, whom we will discuss later. It is important to note that the Evil Eye falls into the same pot of concerns with other life threats.

Another side to the Evil Eye is its malicious casting. Here, Judaism also followed the ancient Greek and Semitic acts of cursing. This included all manner of evil words, even those which were uttered without intention.[205] It need not even be magical words, but simply speaking of misfortune might be enough to result in a curse. Late Judaism, despite deep corruption with superstition and magic, remembered the power of words from the Scriptures.

Other cursing practices even included voodoo dolls. In a curious case, the death of Bishop Eberhard of Treves in 1066 AD was blamed on local Jews who, after bribing a local priest to baptize a wax effigy of the bishop, set it ablaze in a ritual curse.[206]

Christianity and the Evil Eye

Our previous discussions should put an end to any notion that Christianity upholds superstitious beliefs in the Evil Eye. There is no power emanating from the eye, but rather the devil takes advantage of our envious thoughts as a form of demonic prayer and strikes out at our behest.

Magic is strictly forbidden, and those who benefit from it (in the case of visiting Jewish doctors) or who practice it are unanimously condemned. Several examples of this are found in the writings of St. Basil the Great, who said in *Letter 217* (para. 65):

> He who confesses-magic or sorcery shall do penance for the time of murder, and shall be treated in the same manner as he who convicts himself of this sin.

And in *Letter 188* (para. 8), he stated:

On the other hand acts done in the attacks of war or robbery are distinctly intentional, and admit of no doubt. Robbers kill for greed, and to avoid conviction. Soldiers who inflict death in war do so with the obvious purpose not of fighting, nor chastising, but of killing their opponents. And if any one has concocted some magic philter for some other reason, and then causes death, I count this as intentional. Women frequently endeavor to draw men to love them by incantations and magic knots, and give them drugs which dull their intelligence. Such women, when they cause death, though the result of their action may not be what they intended, are nevertheless, on account of their proceedings being magical and prohibited, to be reckoned among intentional homicides. Women also who administer drugs to cause abortion, as well as those who take poisons to destroy unborn children, are murderesses. So much on this subject.

Canon 61 of the 5th Ecumenical Council forbade the use of magic and amulets, and from the writings of the Fathers we know that only the Cross or Gospels are ever worn by believers (c.f. St. John Chrysostom, *Homily 8 on Co 3:5-7*, v. 18 & *Homily 19 on the Statutes to the People of Antioch*, ch. 14; St. Augustine, *Tractate 7*, ch. 6-7 & 12). The blue beads often found on Christians these days fall into the category of magical amulets and are improper. We will give an explanation for the longevity of this belief a bit later.

St. John Chrysostom's catechetical instructions bear witness to the fact that magic beliefs were still strong even within the Christianized Byzantine Empire. These beliefs were often given Christian labels, but based on the same pagan assumptions. At the end of his second instruction, St. John has this to say:

And what is one to say about them who use charms and amulets, and encircle their heads and feet with golden coins of Alexander of Macedon. Are these our hopes, tell me, that after the cross and death of our Master, we should place our hopes of salvation on an image of a Greek king? Dost thou not know what great result the cross has achieved? It has abolished death, has extinguished sin, has made Hades useless, has undone the power of the devil, and is it not worth trusting for the health of the body? It has raised up the whole world, and dost thou not take courage in it? And what wouldest thou be worthy to suffer, tell me? Thou dost not only have amulets always with thee, but incantations bringing drunken and half-witted old women into thine house, and art thou not ashamed, and dost thou not blush, after so great philosophy, to be terrified at such things? and there is a graver thing than this error. For when we deliver these exhortations, and lead them away, thinking that they defend themselves, they say, that the woman is a Christian who makes these incantations, and utters nothing else than the name of God. On this account I especially hate and turn away from her, because she makes use of the name of God, with a view to ribaldry. For even the demons uttered the name of God, but still they were demons, and thus they used to say to Christ, "We know thee who thou art, the Holy One of God," and notwithstanding, he rebuked them, and drove them away. On this account, then, I beseech you to cleanse yourselves from this error, and to keep hold of this word as a staff; and just as without sandals, and cloak, no one of you would choose to go down to the market-place, so without this word never enter the market-place, but when thou art about to pass over the threshold of the gateway, say this word first: I leave thy ranks, Satan, and thy pomp, and thy service, and I join the ranks of Christ. And never go forth without this word. This shall be a staff to thee, this thine armor, this an impregnable fortress, and accompany this word with the sign of the cross on thy forehead. For thus not only a man who meets you, but even the devil himself, will be unable to hurt you at all, when he sees thee everywhere appearing with these weapons; and discipline thyself by these means henceforth, in order that when thou receivest the seal thou mayest be a well-equipped soldier, and planting thy trophy against the devil, may receive the crown of righteousness, which may it be the lot of us all to obtain, through the grace and lovingkindness of our Lord Jesus Christ, with whom be glory to the Father and to the Holy Spirit for ever and ever.

Here, an elderly woman is pictured as using Christ's name as an incantation. Christ's name becomes yet another to add to the 70 used in Jewish magic, and so the saint's ire is raised. To this day, Christian magic is still employed against the Evil Eye in Italy, Greece and the Arab lands.

In some Greek villages, the black and white threads of the Sumerians are still in use.[207] Blue beads, known as 'stopping stones' (*stamatopetra*) because they also allegedly prevent miscarriages, are still employed to avert the Evil Eye. The bead is found in late Judaism, and dates back some 5,000 years to the Assyrians, who installed blue tiles over the gates of their buildings to prevent the Evil Eye.[208] It is considered in general terms a "lucky" bead because it represents water and heaven, both of which are blue. Its light shade of blue (the Turks use cobalt, but Arabs and Greeks prefer a brighter shade closely resembling turquoise) was said to offset the dark phase of the moon and thus limit the powers of Hecate and black magic.[209] The moon was associated with Diana and fertility, and its phases were said to effect lactation and fecundity, and so the blue bead became necessary to offset the 'physics' of the moon (an idea supported by Aristotle) which could also adversely impact young children.[210] In addition, blue sapphire is mentioned in Exodus 24:10 as being under the feet of Yahweh.

We can see now why the Theotokos is often associated with the color blue, and the profundity of blue stones in religious art from the Middle East. The association with fertility has been forgotten, much as the connection between the peacocks in Byzantine-style woodcarving have lost their Evil Eye-preventing purpose[211] and are now merely decorative and 'traditional.' In the case of the blue stones, they served a genuinely constructive purpose, since they allowed the superstitious to draw the conclusion that the Virgin was the example of fertility in bearing the God-man through belief in the Word of God rather than simply functioning in a strictly biological manner. The same probably cannot be said of the peacocks.

In some Greek rural areas, a cross known as a *monokero* (carved by monks on Mt. Athos) is used to heal people suffering from the effects of the Evil Eye.[212] Garlic, bread and even certain saints (esp. St. Stylianos) are considered to be preventatives for the Evil Eye. St. John Chrysostom vociferously condemned the widely-used camouflage tactic of 'soiling,' when mothers smear dirt on their children to avoid the envious eye.[213] Tertullian advised women in church to veil themselves against envious stares and thus avert temptations they would otherwise face, yet his remarks seem to give credence to pagan Evil Eye concepts.[214] Both covering and soiling have been long identified by sociologists as primitive ways of avoiding the Evil Eye, stemming from the natural aversion to being stared at.

Magical prayers and incantations often employed by superstitious Christian people to break the power of the Eye. They almost always employing the name of Christ and the Virgin Mary, and use a variety of materials (nails, live coals, water, etc.) to break the curse. Here is an example of an incantation which follows forty repetitions of the 'Our Father:'

> The cow gave birth to a calf; its mother, licking it, undid the Evil Eye with her spittle.
> And I, the mother, have undone the evil spell by licking. May the child live and prosper and not suffer any harm![215]

Worse still is when rites of divination are used. Divination is often used to diagnose the patient as well as remedy.[216] In the case of many divination rites, oil and water are used.[217] This form of divination is known as lecanomancy, and dates back to ancient Greece.[218] The sad shame it that, despite being condemned by both the Old and New Testaments as well as Ecumenical Councils and the Holy Fathers, divination is so wide-spread that even certain clergy have publicly bragged about their own 'successes' at it.[219] Other clergy, while not practicing the magical aspect, still believe in eye emanations.[220] This is nothing new, considering the examples given by the canonist Balsamon as to the superstitious activities of 12th century clergy.[221]

We have refrained to getting into the gory details of Evil Eye superstitions not out of fear of perpetuating them, but rather to keep the focus on the real problem: a lack of understanding of the Faith or faith in the wrong things. Some Christians ardently believe in Christ, but mix in pagan presuppositions. The Church has long tried to rid people of superstition, with limited success in some cases. Before we become pessimistic, we must realize that a great deal of superstition has been wiped out as well. We are dealing with remnants.

The Cross and the Bead

One remnant is the Evil Eye and fear of child death. We mentioned at the beginning of this book the pagan notion that a first-child ought to be sacrificed to the gods, and that illness in children could be an attempt for the gods to claim the child (rather than a demonic assault). While Jews feared Lilith would attack their children, the Greeks had a fear of Gylou. Gylou was popularly known as a child-stealing demon. Obviously, such murderous intentions were out of envy, and so Greeks employed the same amulets against the Evil Eye as they would against the envious actions of Gylou.

Gylou was actually featured in the hagiography of St. Sisoe, in what turns out to be a fascinating exhibition of the Church's teachings using a pagan motif. In the story, Gylou devoured the children of St. Sisoe's sister and then fled, and so the saint set off to bring the children back.[222] When he finally cornered Gylou, she demanded that St. Sisoe cough up some of his own mother's milk. After asking God's help, he spit up some milk and the defeated demon gave back the children. Here, the saint's miraculous regurgitation is symbolic: Greeks thought that children learned envy during their nursing, and so mothers sought not to 'overween' their children for fear that they will overly desire the milk and become envious later in life. Here, the saint regurgitated, thus showing he was not envious because he was able to share this precious fluid.

So the pagan is surrounded by threats to the life of the child: one from the gods demanding their due, the other from child-stealing demons or negative forces (i.e. moon phases). In either case, the child's life is preserved through fluids: either the blood of a sheep anointed the child (the gods are thus appeased that they have been paid for their gift) or a fluid-symbol amulet kept away dry spirits.

If we apply this thought process to a pagan thinker, we must then ask: what is it about Scripture that explicitly promises that God will not claim the child? Nothing. The child could be "called away" by God at anytime. Obviously, no mother wants her child taken. In her pagan life, she could sacrifice. Now, as a Christian, the only blood that is effective for anything is Christ's. And, the symbol of this is the Cross. The Cross is a symbol of Christ's blood (as THE vicarious sacrifice), and so the Cross comes to replace the blood of sheep for the express purpose of *appeasing* God. If God looks down and sees the Cross, he will be less likely to take the child, at least in the eyes of a pagan.

Thus, the neck cross of an infant can become a tool to keep God away from the child, just as the blood of sheep kept the pagan gods away. Certainly, no saint ever sanctioned such thought, but we can see how easy it is to reason that way. We ask God not to take things from us; it is a request not to act. In refraining, God becomes distant. An unreformed pagan mind is perfectly content with deity at a distance until action is needed. After all, the only reason one believes in any god is through the actions of the god. Action and proximity go hand-in-hand. No one wants a close-by but inactive god.

This is the reason that some people see the need to have a blue bead on the same chain as a cross. The cross keeps God back, while the bead keeps away the other dry spirits. The cross is not intended for the Evil Eye necessarily, but it is only for God. The bead then is still necessary "equipment" to keep the child out of danger from dry spirits.

Charity

A further issue that ought to be addressed is charity. There is an unequivocal requirement in Scripture for Christians to give alms (c.f. De 15:7-11, Mt 5:42 & 19:21, Lu 12:33). However, we must look deeper at the subject of alms, since much ado has been made of not just giving alms but *how* to give them. St. John Chrysostom again is our source, after he made a rather curious argument in his *2nd Catechetical Instruction* (sect. 3) for the moral equality of the maimed and widows to the whole and healthy. In section four, he announced that he accepted all men charged of crimes as Christian brothers. Why did St. John say all these things in an essay that, for the most part, is a condemnation of excessive personal wealth and urges almsgiving? Here we have a key:

"And what are omens?" says one. Often when going forth from his own house he has seen a one-eyed or lame man, and has shunned him as an omen. This is a pomp of Satan. For meeting the man does not make the day turn out ill, but to live in sin. When thou goest forth, then, beware of one thing—that sin does not meet thee. For this it is which trips us up. And without this the devil will be able to do us no harm. What sayest thou? Thou seest a man, and shunnest him as an omen, and dost not see the snare of the devil, how he sets thee at war with him who has done thee no wrong, how he makes thee the enemy of thy brother on no just pretext; but God has bidden us love our enemies; but thou art turned away from him who did thee no wrong, having nothing to charge him with, and dost thou not consider how great is the absurdity, how great the shame, rather how great the danger? Can I speak of anything more absurd? I am ashamed, indeed, and I blush: But for your salvation's sake, I am, I am compelled to speak of it. If a virgin meet him he says the day becomes unsuccessful; but if a harlot meet him, it is propitious, and profitable, and full of much business; are you ashamed? and do you smite your foreheads, and bend to the ground? But do not this on account of the words which I have spoken, but of the deeds which have been done. See then, in this case, how the devil hid his snare, in order that we might turn away from the modest, but salute and be friendly to the unchaste. For since he has heard Christ saying that "He who looketh on a woman to desire her, has already committed adultery with her," and has seen many get the better of unchastity, wishing by another wrong to cast them again into sin, by this superstitious observance he gladly persuades them to pay attention to whorish women.[223]

In St. John's world, the very people Christians are called to give alms to were avoided out of fear of their envious Evil Eye. Beggars and widows were thought to be envious of the well, and so people did their best to avoid them. The profits of begging were not as much out of compassion as fear, since the superstitious were concerned that a scorned beggar would curse them.[224]

This is probably one of the reasons fear is mentioned in connection with giving alms in 2 Corinthians 9:7. In this chapter, St. Paul associated charity as a "lucky" activity for those with superstitious tendencies. He explained how God gives all things, and that He enjoys our giving and rewards it with giving of His own (vv. 8-11). Yet, just so that the less superstitious are aware of what he is doing, St. Paul referred to such giving as "service" and "obedience" (vv. 12-13). Rather than averting disaster and bad luck, almsgiving is presented in the Scripture as a positive activity and one that should not involve fear.

Solomon, St. George and the Evil Eye

One curiosity worth mentioning before concluding this book is the parallel between St. George and King Solomon. The reader most likely would find this subject utterly irrelevant in light of what we have already discussed, but there is in fact a historical connection between the fear of the Evil Eye and the seeming omnipresence of St. George in the Orthodox world. Without delving into great detail, we will discuss the connection in history to show a successful effort by the Church to Christianize a pagan symbol so thoroughly that its former meaning has been utterly forgotten.

According to the tradition of St. George preserved in the Orthodox Church, the martyrdom of St. George occurred around 304 AD, though the exact location is under contention to this day.[225] While the most common versions of the *legenda* indicate Nicomedia, scholars believe this is a later addition to the original text (along with the mentioning of Diocletian by name).[226] Eusebius of Caesarea mentions a martyrdom in Nicodemia by Diocletian, but does not give a name.[227]

Actual historical data on St. George is scant. As far back as 495 AD, when Pope Gelasius issued his edict calling into question the various tales of St. George, there has been much argument as to his existence or the biographical accuracy of his many legends. In the case of the pope, he found the many tales so outrageous that he added one *legenda* to his *Index* of heretical documents (the first such ban of writings in church history) and declared that the Church of Rome would only ascribe to five tortures, three miracles and a total omission of any resurrections from death.[228]

Joppa was most likely to be his birthplace, given that St. Constantine the Great built the basilica there over the saint's relics not 20 years after his martyrdom. Documents from the deacon Theodosios in 530 describe the healings associated with the relics there.[229] A problem for historians has been the rather late appearance of documentation describing pilgrimages to the tomb in Joppa. Between the saint's martyrdom in 304 and Theodosios' description of the pilgrimage in 530 leaves a sizable gap. What hagiographers note is that there appears to be such gaps between times with all of the military martyrs[230] and this makes St. George typical in that respect.

The final story in the collection of St. George's miracles is that of slaying the dragon, set in the mountains of Lebanon near Beirut. In this instance, a dragon has been terrifying a town, and so the king ordered (on the instruction of their pagan gods) that each family, in turn, must leave a daughter on the shore of the lake from which the dragon comes. Finally, the king's own daughter is placed on the shore. As she awaits the beast, St. George appeared. She tried to convince him to leave but he refuses, saying that in the name of the Lord he will kill the dragon. When it appeared, he thrusted his spear through the dragon's mouth. Ordering the princess to tie the dragon with her sash, and they led it into the city like a dog. After preaching Christ, he killed the dragon and baptizes 25,000 male inhabitants of the town. After leaving, the people erect a church in honor of the Virgin and St. George, out of which a miraculous spring flows.[231]

In the East, dragon stories were attributed to several military saints including St. Theodore. The earliest documentation of the dragon dates to the early 10th century from Simon Metaphrastes, who used it metaphorically to describe the saint's struggle with the devil.[232] Coupled with the iconographic representation dating as far back as the 11th century, we can see where the Crusaders, who spread the fame of St. George throughout Europe.

In the West, the dragon story appeared in a late thirteenth century in what proved to be the world's first "best-selling book," the *Legenda Sanctorum*. Composed by the bishop of Genoa,[233] this book gained wide recognition as an exceptional collection of saints' lives. Here, the bishop warned that the Council of Nicea had declared there to be no certainty of St. George's actual existence (possibly some confusion exists between this council, which did not mention the saint, and Pope Gelasius' contention in 495). Yet, he quoted St. Ambrose of Milan's praises of St. George, which is historically accurate and quite helpful in placing the saint in reality.[234] This tale placed St. George as a tribune in the Roman Army, riding through Silena in Libya (apparently before his martyrdom). In the end of the tale, when offered the hand of the maiden by the king, he instead took leave of them. Later European commentators appeared to regain something of the Byzantine version, citing St. George as powerful example of overcoming the devil (symbolized by the serpent), but the story by then was seen more as literal than figurative.[235]

Aside from appearing by name in nearly every service's dismissal prayer and in the proskomedia commemoration, St. George has his own feast day. Because of the date, his feast can fall anywhere between the end of Great Lent and the Pentecostal season. This makes his service both tricky to set up and also one of special priority, since the rubrics preserve much of his material during this season even on days of Holy Week. Should the feast fall on Great Saturday or Pascha, rather than disappear, the feast is transferred to Bright Monday, which is highly unusual for a saint's feast.[236] No mention is made of his exploits with the dragon, which suggest that this part of his *legenda* is both late and not entirely accepted by the Church.

There is a rich tradition of iconographic patterns for St. George, and one need not try hard to find the many ways the saint is portrayed. Generally speaking, the earliest icons of St. George are portraits without a horse, often holding a spear and shield. Sometimes, he is seen gripping a sword or even a duplicate of his own head. Much as would like to, for the sake of time I must limit this to the Eastern tradition and ignore many interesting points regarding the portrayal of St. George in the West.

By the 11th century, St. George received his horse and dragon. The earliest portrayals on horseback have been found in churches in Goreme, Turkey, dating to the 11th century,[237] a century after Simon Metaphrases' metaphorical writings of the dragon as a picture of Satan. There soon after appears the princess and the king and the village. One can easily come to the conclusion that the dragon story is a much later addition to the life of St. George, and is in fact inconsequential to his sanctity.

What troubles historians is catholicity of dragon stories throughout Europe and how St. George fits into this. Dragons reports seem to be an unquestioned part of life in antiquity, judging by their sheer number: the *Tarasque de Noves* in Avignon, the *Kraulla* in Rheims, the *Gran' Gueule* in Poitiers, the *Gargouille* of Rouen (whence comes the word "gargoyle"), the *Tarasque* of Tarascon, the dragon of Wantley and the "worms" at Bishop Auckland and Lambton.[238] The last account of a dragon is in the 17th century in St. Leonard's Forest in Horsham, England. If aquatic beasts were to be counted (which also could be an interpretation of the dragon given that the beast came from a lake) then the list would be much longer without relying on the relatively modern Loch Ness monster.[239] To the masses of peasants troubled by such beasts, St. George was an all the more a sympathetic character.

Greek mythology was full of dragon-slaying heroes: Zeus versus the Typhon, Apollo versus the Python of Delphi, Herakles versus the Geryon and the Hydra (on separate occasions), Bellerphon versus the Chimaera, Kadmus versus the dragon, Ulysses versus the Scylla and Jason versus the dragon guarding the Golden Fleece.[240] The dragon story itself has been compared as a take-off on the tale of Persius and Andromeda, and is quite similar in enough ways to make the Christian takeover of a pagan myth quite plausible. In fact, both legends are said to have taken place within miles of one another (Perseus in Joppa, Israel; St. George in Lydda, Lebanon). However, scholars do note the veneration of the saint long before the dragon story became widely known, and scholars can find no connection between the two as far as the veneration of the saint goes.[241] So, what is the connection between St. George and the dragon?

The connection is Solomon. Pre-Christian iconography depicted Solomon as riding a horse and slaying a dragon,[242] something that was described in some of the apocryphal stories of Solomon in Hellenized Semitic world. We have a great deal of archeological evidence labeling the rider as Solomon,[243] and it would appear that the image of St. George was a direct take-over. This might have been developing for some time, given that St. John of Damascus' 8th century hymn to St. George appears to make a connection between Solomon and St. George some two hundred years before the completion of the takeover.[244]

But, what is the importance of Solomon in regards to the Evil Eye? Very simply, Solomon was a central figure in Hellenized Judeo-Christian magic.[245] Josephus testified to the Jewish beliefs that Solomon possessed powers as an exorcist and healer of demonic oppression.[246] In the apocryphal book *The Testament of Solomon*, God gave Solomon power over the demons, whom he then employed to build his Temple. In the story, he captured and interviewed a number of spirits, and the document becomes a teaching tool of demonology. In the tale, Beelzeboul is said to inspire envy in men, but there is also a headless demon named Envy.[247] This headless demon saw by his feelings, and stole men's mental abilities. He also afflicted small children and appeared closely related to the envious Gylou. Solomon bound this demon and set him to work on the Temple.

The issue of headlessness does not end here. St. George's tomb was often used for the incubation of maniacs, and the chains used to secure patients were later mistakenly thought to be those of his imprisonment.[248] Apparently, this attribute to St. George came from his connection to Solomon and the notion that madness was a demonic affliction, since nothing can be seen in his hagiography that would otherwise indicate his special compassion for those who have 'lost their minds.' Or, should we say, 'heads?'

In ancient magic, Solomon is often invoked for assistance against headless spirits.[249] It would appear than many people had a concern for headless beings based on archeological evidence. If stealing heads is motivated out of envy, then we can assume that headless beings and those seeking heads are envious. We already know that St. George was beheaded, but we ought not forget that St. John the Forerunner was also beheaded. Both executions, it seems, were motivated out of *hybris* because both saints decreased the honor of royalty. We suggest that St. John's manner of execution fit well with the theme of envy, since beheading suggests both *hybris* and envy.

Solomon/St. George's white horse also follows a long tradition of symbology: the horse was often a symbol found on the tombs of martyrs. Its white hair as a sign of purity according to some scholars, and the horse personified the strength martyrs needed to endure their hardship.[250] But, more importantly, the horse was a symbol of defeat of the serpent. If we recall our Old Testament discussions of the serpent and the horse, then this symbol makes sense. The serpent (or basilisk) is a symbol of envy, and Solomon's magic binds and defeats the power of envy. Some amulets of Solomon depict him piercing a woman or woman/serpent combination often identified as Lilith.[251]

There is also an Islamic connection. *El Khedir* (the 'Green One,' which is a popular epithet for St. George) is a venerated saint amongst the Moslems, whom they report to have drunk from the fountain of immortality and is a help for those with fertility problems. Further, the Sufi sect believes he is analogous to St. Elijah and lived at the time of Moses, with backing from the Koran that states El Khedir actually gave the Law to Moses.[252] Solomon appears in the Koran (however, not as El Khedir) as having special powers over the demonic.[253]

It appears that El Khedir's identification with St. George as another "takeover identity," much as St. George took over either Perseus' or Dionysus' identity in many parts of Greece. Today, one finds many of St. George's shrines next to or replaced by mosques devoted to El Khedir. Considering the great force of St. George's cult in the region, the Turks may have found this as a way to compromise with their new Christian population after the fall of Byzantium.[254] We can tell that the takeover is much later, since the Muslims treat Solomon as a separate entity and preserve his influence over the demonic.

So, we can see the tremendous success of the Church in wiping out the cult of Solomon by taking over one of its most powerful symbols: the rider. While superstition and magic have never completely departed the scene, this instance is remarkable in that the memory of Solomon's magic and the original message of the rider icon was utterly replaced. This is obvious, considering that the image of St. George, while pervasive, is no longer specially connected to repelling demons any more than any other icon, nor it St. George called upon to bind the powers of the Evil Eye as Solomon was before.

Conclusion

Based on the information presented, we can arrive at the following conclusions:

- Envy has played a part in human dynamics from earliest history, especially is the Semitic world.

- Envy is a major theme in the Law, Psalms, and Prophets, as well as the New Testament.

- The Old Testament develops the premise that Yahweh has created unlimited good and fertility, thus eliminating the need for natural religions that seek to add fertility and luck to people and things.

- Scripture combines envy with jealousy, covetousness and stinginess into a single concept that is a manifestation of idolatry of the self and belief that there is a limited supply of good.

- Envy/covetousness ultimately leads to murder.

- It is only through bloodshed that one can repent of sin, and so the Law mandates sacrifice as a way of preventing murder.

- The Exodus is always motivated by Scapegoating, when people project their sins upon the one chosen by God.

- Christ's earthly ministry centered on convicting the world of idolatry by provoking people (represented by the Pharisees) to envy and then murder.

- By becoming the scapegoat, Christ allows us to place our sins upon Him, so that we might repent at the sight of His blood.

- The Cross is a messenger of mankind's envy and murderous intentions.

- Envy will drive men even so far as to attempt murder on God (theocide).

- The Holy Fathers consistently opposed superstitious beliefs in the Evil Eye and magical practices, upholding the Scriptural understanding of envy and vision.

Having come to this point, we must ask what the Evil Eye means to the modern man. Why is it important? What will seeing envy in the Scriptures add to our understanding of the Gospel message?

Frankly, envy takes us beyond morality and 'right-versus-wrong' to a world of 'survival-versus-destruction.' The Law of Moses was not about pleasing God but guaranteeing the continuation of the human race. Envy represents a suicidal streak in mankind, a desire to destroy himself and his world when he cannot be God. Morality teaches us that right and wrong are differentiated by rewards and punishments meted out by a higher authority (i.e., God, society, parents, etc.). To some degree morality is also arbitrary, since we know that what is 'right' in one culture can be 'wrong' in another. Envy is not a moral issue: no one can punish the envious more than he has already suffered at his own hands, nor has any society permitted unrestrained envy as a good. Morals have regulated the permissible expressions of envy, but envy somehow lies beyond the reach of ethics. Actions can be governed and eliminated, but base impulses can only be covered up and unacknowledged.

Envy is a law, a governing principle just like those found in physical sciences. It follows a predictable path of destruction. There are no categories of 'good envy' and 'bad envy' by which it could be differentiated. It is simple like gravity. Gravity has complex causes as does envy, but its effects are straightforward. Envy is no different. It kills and destroys as its natural function.

Therefore, we are obligated to search ourselves for envy and eliminate its root cause: idolatrous self-centeredness. Envy itself cannot be harnessed, nor can it be 'converted' or 'baptized' into something good. Its gnawing teeth cannot be ignored. Envy can only be eliminated by attacking the conditions that brought it about, just as stopping the rotation of an object in space will eliminate its gravitational field.

If we fail to acknowledge and deal with our own personal envy, we will inevitably destroy something or someone. The rampage of this passion will not cease until it has tasted blood. Sadly, the only blood envy recognizes is the blood of those possessed by it. Judas was not satisfied with even the blood of God, his passion was only quenched with his own vital fluid.

The tragedy of the fall is that man lost his introspection. Judas had no hope of looking within himself and seeing his envy. It took the shedding of blood for him to see himself for what he was. Our only hope is to see the Crucifixion of Christ as an image of our own envious desires. The Cross as preached in the Word of God is the mirror by which we see ourselves as the murderers and idolaters that we are.

The only resources man has for salvation from envy are to be found within the true Christian Tradition (I believe is what the Orthodox Church is), which helps each person establish a spiritual manner of living that leads to a relationship with God.

Without this relationship, the world is a place of limited good and constant risk. Envy is almost a natural response. However, to a genuine Christian, one who walks in the traditions of the Apostles (those who knew and learned from Jesus Christ), sees envy as the culmination of deception. Envy is the fruit of the lie. It is a rejection of the truth that God provides all things and is infinitely just in all His ways. It is militant blindness to the good found within each of us and in the whole of Creation.

The Christian message is thus: man will destroy himself through envy if he does not set aside his selfishness and acknowledge God's unlimited goodness. It is through this pivotal realization that man turns from his personal Hell and enters the free gift of God's Paradise.

Bibliography

al-Ashqar, Umar Sulaiman. *The World of the Jinn and Devils.* Translated by Zarabozo, Jamaal. Boulder, CO: al-Basheer Company for Publications and Translations, 1998.

anonymous. *Testament of Solomon* [web page]. Peterson, Joseph H., March 18, 1999 1st—3rd c. AD [cited March 29 2000]. Available from http://www.avesta.org/solomon/testamen.htm.

Antiochian Orthodox Christian Archdiocese of North America, ed. *Service Book of the Holy Eastern Orthodox Catholic and Apostolic Church.* 1993 ed. Englewood, NJ: Antiochian Orthodox Christian Archdiocese of North America, 1971.

Bauer, Walter, William F. Arndt, F. Wilbur Gingrich, and Frederick W. Danker. *A Greek-English Lexicon of the New Testament and Other Early Christian Literature.* Chicago: University of Chicago Press, 1957.

Billington, Clyde E. Jr. *Evidence of Canaanite Child Sacrifice Found on Sardinia* Northwestern College Center for Distance Education, 1997 [cited. Available from http://www.nwc.edu/disted/his317/unit6/read6_5.htm.

Breck, John. "Chiasmus as a Key to Biblical Interpretation." *St. Vladimir's Theological Quarterly* 42, no. 3-4 (1999): 249-267.

Brown, Francis, S. R. Driver, and Charles A. Briggs. *The Brown-Driver-Briggs Hebrew and English Lexicon.* 1996 ed. Peabody, MA: Hendrickson Publishers, 1906.

Burke, Joseph. *The Tyranny of Malice: Exploring the Dark Side of Character.* New York: Summit Books, 1988.

Casalis, Matthieu. "The Dry and the Wet: a Semiological Analysis of Creation and Flood Myths." *Semiotica* 17, no. 1 (1976): 35-67.

Chadwick, Henry. *The Early Church.* 1993 ed. New York: Penguin Books, 1967.

Constantinides, Evagoras, ed. *Mikron Evchologion i Agiasmatarion*. Merrillville, IN: Evagoras Constantinides, 1989.

Coss, Richard G. "Reflections on the Evil Eye." In *The Evil Eye: a Casebook*, edited by Alan Dundes, 181-191. Madison, WI: University of Wisconsen Press, 1974.

Drimeyer, Jack. "Conversation with Father Lawdis." *Hellenic Chronicle*, 4 April 1974, 6.

Dunbabin, Katherine M. D., and M. W. Dickie. "Invidia Rumpantur Pectora: The Iconography of Phthonos/Invidia In Graeco-Roman Art." *JAC*, no. 26 (1983): 7-37.

Dundes, Alan. "Wet and Dry, the Evil Eye: an Essay in Indo-European and Semitic Worldview." In *The Evil Eye: A Casebook*, edited by Alan Dundes, 257-312. Madison, WI: The University of Wisconsin Press, 1981.

Elliott, John H. "The Evil Eye and the Sermon on the Mount." *Biblical Interpretation* 2, no. 1 (1994): 51-84.

Elworthy, Frederick Thomas. *The Evil Eye: An Account of This Ancient and Widespread Superstition*. 1986 ed. New York: Julian Press, 1895.

Fögen, Marie T. "Balsamon on Magic: From Roman Secular Law to Byzantine Canon Law." In *Byzantine Magic*, edited by Henry Maguire, 99-115. Washington, DC: Dunbarton Oaks, 1995.

Foster, George. "The Anatomy of Envy: A Study of Symbolic Behavior." *Current Anthropology* 13, no. 2 (1972): 165-186.

Foster, George. "Peasant Society and the Image of the Limited Good." *American Anthropologist* 67 (1965): 293-315.

Gordon, Richard. "Imagining Greek and Roman Magic." In *Witchcraft and Magic in Europe: Ancient Greece and Rome*, edited by Bengt Ankarloo and Stuart Clark. Philadelphia: University of Pennsylvania, 1999.

Graf, Fritz. *Magic in the Ancient World*. Translated by Philip, Franklin. Edited by G. W. Bowersock. Vol. 10, *Revealing Antiquity*. Cambridge, MA: Harvard University Press, 1997.

Gravel, Pierre Bettez. The Malevolent Eye: an Essay on the Evil Eye, Fertility and the Concept of Mana. Vol. 64, American University Studies, Series XI—Anthropology and Sociology. New York: Peter Lang, 1995.

Hagedorn, Anselm C., and Jerome H. Neyrey. *"It Was Out of Envy That They Handed Jesus Over" (Mark 15:10): The Anatomy of Envy and the Gospel of Mark* 1999 [cited 03/28/00 2000]. Available from http://www.nd.edu/~jneyrey1/envy.html.

Hardie, Margaret M. "The Evil Eye in Some Greek Villiages of the Upper Haliakmon Valley in West Macedonia." In *The Evil Eye: A Casebook*, edited by Alan Dundes, 107-123. Madison, WI: University of Wisconsen Press, 1923.

Harfouche, Jamal K. "The Evil Eye and Infant Health in Lebanon." In *The Evil Eye: A Casebook*, edited by Alan Dundes, 86-106. Madison, WI: University of Wisconsen Press, 1965.

Holy Trinity Monastery, ed. *The Passion and Miracles of the Great Martyr and Victorious Wonderworker Saint George*. 1957 ed. Jordanville, NY: Holy Trinity Monastery, 1957.

Johnson, Luke T. "The New Testament's Anti-Jewish Slander and the Conventions of the Ancient Polemic." *Journal of Biblical Literature* 108, no. 3 (1989): 419-441.

Joines, Karen R. "The Serpent in Gen 3." *Zeitschrift für die Alttestamentliche Wissenschaft* 87, no. 1 (1975): 1-11.

Levenson, Jon D. *The Death and Resurrection of the Beloved Son: The Transformation of Child Sacrifice and Christianity*. New Haven, CT: Yale University Press, 1993.

Lloyd, G. E. R. "The Hot and the Cold, the Wet and the Dry in Greek Philosophy." *The Journal of Hellenic Studies* LXXXIV (1964): 92-106.

Louth, Andrew. "Envy as the Chief Sin in Athanasius and Gregory of Nyssa." *Studia Patristica* 15, no. 1 (1980): 458-460.

Luck, Georg. "Witches and Sorcerers in Classical Literature." In *Witchcraft and Magic in Europe: Ancient Greece and Rome*, edited by Bengt Ankarloo and Stuart Clark. Philadelphia: University of Pennsylvania, 1999.

Mackay, Christopher S. *Carthage* 1999 [cited June 1 2000]. Available from http://www.ualberta.ca/~csmackay/CLASS_365/Carthage.html.

Meyer, Marvin. "Greek Texts of Ritual Power from Christian Egypt." In *Ancient Christian Magic*, edited by Marvin Meyer, Richard Smith and Neal Kelsey, 28-57. San Francisco: HarperCollins Publishers, 1994.

Migliore, Sam. *Mal'uocchiu: Ambiguity, Evil Eye, and the Language of Distress.* Toronto: University of Toronto Press, 1997.

Nassar, Seraphim, ed. *Divine Prayers and Services of the Catholic Orthodox Church of Christ.* 1993 ed. Englwood, NJ: Antiochian Orthodox Christian Archdiocese of North America, 1938.

Neyrey, Jerome. *Questions, Chreai, and Challenges to Honor. The Interface of Rhetoric and Culture in Mark's Gospel* 1998 [cited 1 October 2000]. Available from http://www.nd.edu/~jneyrey1/questions.html.

Onians, Richard Broxton. *The Origins of European Thought About the Body, the Mind, the Soul, the World, Time and Fate.* 1981 ed. Cambridge: Cambridge University Press, 1951.

Pardee, Dennis. "Muerôrat-Puetanîm "venom" in Job 20:14." *Zeitschrift für die Alttestamentliche Wissenschaft* 19, no. 3 (1979): 401-416.

Parrott, W. Gerrod. "The Emotional Experiences of Envy and Jealousy." In *The Psychology of Jealousy and Envy*, edited by Peter Salovey, 3-30. New York: Guilford Press, 1991.

Random House, ed. *Webster's Encyclopedic Unabridged Dictionary.* 1996 ed. New York: Gramercy Books, 1987.

Roberts, John M. "Belief in the Evil Eye in World Perspective." In *The Evil Eye*, edited by Clarence Maloney, 223-265. New York: Columbia University Press, 1976.

Russell, Jeffrey B. *Satan: The Early Christian Tradition.* 1994 ed. Ithaca, NY: Cornell University Press, 1981.

Schoeck, Helmut. *Envy. A Theory of Social Behavior.* Translated by Glenny, Michael Ross, Betty. 1970 ed. New York: Harcourt, Brace and World, Inc., 1966.

Schrire, Theodore. *Hebrew Magic Amulets.* 1982 ed. New York: Behrman House, Inc., 1966.

Scott Fox, David. *Saint George: The Saint With Three Faces.* Windor Forest, Bershire, UK: The Kensal Press, 1983.

Siebers, Tobin. *The Mirror of Medusa.* Los Angeles: University of California Press, 1983.

Singer, Erwin. *Key Concepts in Psychotherapy.* Second ed. Northvale, NJ: Jason Aronson, Inc., 1965.

Smith, Louis. "Original is as 'Envy': The Structure of the Biblical Decalogue." *Dialog* 30, no. 3 (1991): 227-230.

St. Athanasius of Alexandria. "Against the Heathen, Part 2." In *The AGES Digital Library [CD-ROM]*, edited by Archibald Robinson. Albany, OR: AGES Software, 321.

St. Athanasius of Alexandria. "In Defense of His Flight." In *The AGES Digital Library [CD-ROM]*, edited by Archibald Robinson. Albany, OR: AGES Software, 360.

St. Basil the Great. "On Jealousy and Envy." In *St. Basil—Ascetical Works.* New York: Fathers of the Early Church, Inc., 370.

St. Cyprian of Carthage. "On Envy." In *The AGES Digital Library [CD-ROM]*, edited by Alexander Roberts and James Donaldson. Albany, OR: AGES Software, 270.

St. Gregory of Nyssa. *The Life of Moses.* Translated by Malherbe, Abaraham J. Ferguson, Everett. Edited by Richard J. Payne. 1978 ed, *Classics of Western Spirituality.* New York: Paulist Press, 390.

St. Gregory of Nyssa. "Oration on Meletius." In *Select Writings and Letters of Gregory, Bishop of Nyssa*, edited by William Moore and Henry A. Wilson. Ann Arbor, MI: Malloy, Inc., 381.

St. Irenaeus of Lyons. "Against Heresies, Book 5." In *The AGES Digital Library [CD-ROM]*, edited by Alexander Roberts and James Donaldson. Albany, OR: AGES Software, 200.

St. John Chrysostom. "Second Instruction to the Catechumens." In *The AGES Digital Library [CD-ROM]*, edited by Philip Schaff. Albany, OR: AGES Software, 400.

St. Tikhon's Monastery, ed. *The Great Book of Needs*. Vol. I—The Holy Mysteries. South Canaan, PA: St. Tikhon's Seminary Press, 1998.

Stanmeyer, Anastasia. "Evil Eye." *The Tampa Tribune*, February 26 1995, 12.

Tarazi, Paul N. *The New Testament: An Introduction*. Vol. 1—Paul and Mark. Crestwood, NY: St. Vladimir's Seminary Press, 1999.

Tarazi, Paul N. *The Old Testament: An Introduction*. Vol. 1—Historical Traditions. Crestwood, NY: St. Vladimir's Seminary Press, 1991.

Tertullian. "On the Veiling of Virgins." In *The AGES Digital Library [CD-ROM]*, edited by Alexander Roberts and James Donaldson. Albany, OR: AGES Software, 200.

Thomsen, Marie-Louise. "The Evil Eye in Mesopotamia." *Journal of Near East Studies*, no. 51 (1992): 19-32.

Trachtenberg, Joshua. *Jewish Magic and Superstition*. 1987 ed. New York: Atheneum, 1939.

Ulmer, Rikva. *The Evil Eye in the Bible and Rabbinic Literature*. Hoboken, NJ: KTAV Publishing House, 1994.

Walcot, Peter. *Envy and the Greeks: A study of human behavior*. Warminster, UK: Aris and Phillips, Ltd., 1978.

Waldman, Nahum M. : 199-203.

Yamauchi, Edwin M. *Persia and the Bible*. 1996 ed. Grand Rapids, MI: Baker Book House Co., 1990.

Zajonc, Arthur. *Catching the Light: the Entwined History of Light and Mind.* 1995 ed. New York: Oxford University Press, 1993.

Endnotes

1. Random House, ed. *Webster's Encyclopedic Unabridged Dictionary.* 1996 ed. New York: Gramercy Books, 1987., p. 672

2. ibid., p. 700

3. ibid., p. 1382

4. Bauer, Walter, William F. Arndt, F. Wilbur Gingrich, and Frederick W. Danker. *A Greek-English Lexicon of the New Testament and Other Early Christian Literature.* Chicago: University of Chicago Press, 1957., p. 137

5. ibid., p. 137

6. ibid., p. 137

7. Brown, Francis, S. R. Driver, and Charles A. Briggs. *The Brown-Driver-Briggs Hebrew and English Lexicon.* 1996 ed. Peabody, MA: Hendrickson Publishers, 1906., p. 888

8. ibid., p. 948

9. Schoeck, Helmut. *Envy. A Theory of Social Behavior.* Translated by Glenny, Michael Ross, Betty. 1970 ed. New York: Harcourt, Brace and World, Inc., 1966.

10. Roberts, John M. "Belief in the Evil Eye in World Perspective." In *The Evil Eye*, edited by Clarence Maloney, 223-265. New York: Columbia University Press, 1976., p. 229

11. Random House, 1987, p. 650

12. Schoeck, 1966, pp. 1-6

13. ibid.

14. ibid., pp. 26-31

15. Schoeck, 1966; Burke, Joseph. *The Tyranny of Malice: Exploring the Dark Side of Character.* New York: Summit Books, 1988.; Dundes, Alan. "Wet and Dry, the Evil Eye: an Essay in Indo-European and Semitic World-

view." In *The Evil Eye: A Casebook*, edited by Alan Dundes, 257-312. Madison, WI: The University of Wisconsen Press, 1981.

16. Burke, 1988, p. 60

17. Burke, 1988, p. 70

18. Parrott, W. Gerrod. "The Emotional Experiences of Envy and Jealousy." In *The Psychology of Jealousy and Envy*, edited by Peter Salovey, 3-30. New York: Guilford Press, 1991., pp. 15-17

19. Coss, Richard G. "Reflections on the Evil Eye." In *The Evil Eye: a Casebook*, edited by Alan Dundes, 181-191. Madison, WI: University of Wisconsen Press, 1974.

20. Random House, 1987, p. 466

21. Foster, George. "The Anatomy of Envy: A Study of Symbolic Behavior." *Current Anthropology* 13, no. 2 (1972): 165-186., p. 168

22. St. Basil the Great. "On Jealousy and Envy." In *St. Basil—Ascetical Works*. New York: Fathers of the Early Church, Inc., 370.

23. Thomsen, Marie-Louise. "The Evil Eye in Mesopotamia." *Journal of Near East Studies*, no. 51 (1992): 19-32.

24. Thomsen, 1992

25. Zajonc, Arthur. *Catching the Light: the Entwined History of Light and Mind*. 1995 ed. New York: Oxford University Press, 1993., pp. 21-22

26. ibid., pp. 29-31

27. Gordon, Richard. "Imagining Greek and Roman Magic." In *Witchcraft and Magic in Europe: Ancient Greece and Rome*, edited by Bengt Ankarloo and Stuart Clark. Philadelphia: University of Pennsylvania, 1999., pp. 221-222

28. Zajonc, 1993, pp. 29-32

29. ibid., p. 31

30. Siebers, Tobin. *The Mirror of Medusa*. Los Angeles: University of California Press, 1983., pp. 62-65

31. Dundes, Alan. "Wet and Dry, the Evil Eye: an Essay in Indo-European and Semitic Worldview." In *The Evil Eye: A Casebook*, edited by Alan

Dundes, 257-312. Madison, WI: The University of Wisconsen Press, 1981., pp. 257-312

32. Yamauchi, Edwin M. *Persia and the Bible.* 1996 ed. Grand Rapids, MI: Baker Book House Co., 1990.

33. Onians, Richard Broxton. *The Origins of European Thought About the Body, the Mind, the Soul, the World, Time and Fate.* 1981 ed. Cambridge: Cambridge University Press, 1951.

34. Foster, George. "Peasant Society and the Image of the Limited Good." *American Anthropologist* 67 (1965): 293-315., p. 300

35. The latter raises a question: do primitive peoples understand the power of the Evil Eye to be *logikos?* There appears to be a great deal of ambiguity in regards to this question, which we shall address later.

36. Lloyd, G. E. R. "The Hot and the Cold, the Wet and the Dry in Greek Philosophy." *The Journal of Hellenic Studies* LXXXIV (1964): 92-106., pp. 92-93

37. Onians, Richard Broxton. *The Origins of European Thought About the Body, the Mind, the Soul, the World, Time and Fate.* 1981 ed. Cambridge: Cambridge University Press, 1951., p. 31

38. ibid., p. 213

39. Dundes, 1981, pp. 266-267

40. Onians, 1951, pp. 254-270

41. The numerous Old Testament reference to God bringing life out of dry places specifically refutes this wet/dry dualism: God consistently makes the dry places sources of life in the Exodus theme.

42. Onians, 1951, pp. 254-270

43. Levenson, Jon D. *The Death and Resurrection of the Beloved Son: The Transformation of Child Sacrifice and Christianity.* New Haven, CT: Yale University Press, 1993.

44. Billington, Clyde E. Jr. *Evidence of Canaanite Child Sacrifice Found on Sardinia* Northwestern College Center for Distance Education, 1997 [cited. Available from http://www.nwc.edu/disted/his317/unit6/read6_5.htm.

Mackay, Christopher S. *Carthage* 1999 [cited June 1 2000]. Available from http://www.ualberta.ca/~csmackay/CLASS_365/Carthage.html.

45. Levenson, 1993, pp. 23-24

46. Gravel, Pierre Bettez. *The Malevolent Eye: an Essay on the Evil Eye, Fertility and the Concept of Mana.* Vol. 64, *American University Studies, Series XI—Anthropology and Sociology.* New York: Peter Lang, 1995., pp. 39-42

47. As we have discussed before, a childless woman is a curse in Near East culture. The inability to produce offspring is certain to destabilize the community by failing to provide an inheritor to the family estate or provide for the sterile couple in their old age. As we have already discussed, infertility is contrary to nature. Yahweh explicitly creates a fertile world, but man's disobedience leads to infertility. So, infertility is seen as an aspect of the Fall, or imposition by God upon a couple. Purposeful sterility is specifically condemned in the Old Testament (c.f. De 25:5-12 and Ge 38).

In terms of superstition, the Evil Eye is linked with sterility, both in terms of endangering pregnancy as well as engendering envy in the barren. The first case is with Sarah, who eyed Hagar in her pregnancy (which some rabbis account for her losing the first child). Rachel also envied Leah after she had given Jacob three sons (Ge 30:1).

In both of these cases, the cause of sterility is implied in their reactions to another's pregnancy. Hagar and Leah both had faith in Yahweh to give them justice for being maltreated, and that justice was the mercy of bearing sons. Their fertility was not in question, but rather being the mother of the heir to the family name, which implies legal protection (i.e., they could not be disowned or divorced and left to their own devices).

We must then look at the three women who were infertile: Sarah, Rebekah and Rachel. We have added to this list Rebekah because she only bore two sons in a single pregnancy, and that Esau, in selling his birthright, is no longer a son). To be only pregnant once in a marriage is also a tenuous situation given the average life expectancy and infant mortality rate of the ancient world. Women were expected to bear as many children as possible to guarantee that at least a few would be healthy enough in adulthood to maintain the family properties and carry on the name.

Of course, each of these women did conceive a son, and a special son at that. Their barrenness is a sign that God has interfered with their normal fertility to show His special intervention in conception. Adam noted that God helped him and Eve conceive Cain (Ge 4:1), and it is explicit in the Law that everything belongs to God in the first place. God guarantees and protects the fertility He imbued creation with. For God to interfere with fertility means He intends to draw special attention to the single child.

Therefore, barrenness is not strictly an evil, but is at best ambiguous in Biblical terms. The Scriptures do acknowledge that it triggers envy, but at the same time prevents us from assuming that it is only a curse. It can be a sign that God is acting especially with the barren woman, and that denunciations of her "Evil Eye" might also fit into the previous discussion of false accusation and scapegoating. This makes barrenness a sign of God's favor, that He plans a special "fruit" from the empty womb. This could also be a theme of Christian monasticism, which emphasizes physical abstinence as a way of setting one's self aside for this special birthing: spiritual children.

48. Foster, 1965, p. 301

49. Bauer, 1957, p. 337

50. Walcot, Peter. *Envy and the Greeks: A study of human behavior.* Warminster, UK: Aris and Phillips, Ltd., 1978., pp. 2-3

51. ibid., p. 2

52. ibid., p. 14

53. ibid., p. 14

54. ibid., p. 14

55. ibid., p. 13

56. ibid., p. 16-21

57. Hagedorn, Anselm C., and Jerome H. Neyrey. *"It Was Out of Envy That They Handed Jesus Over" (Mark 15:10): The Anatomy of Envy and the Gospel of Mark* 1999 [cited 03/28/00 2000]. Available from http://www.nd.edu/~jneyrey1/envy.html., p. 5

58. ibid., p. 5

59. Walcot, 1978, p. 18

60. ibid., p. 16

61. ibid., p. 17

62. ibid., pp. 39-40

63. ibid., p. 40

64. ibid., p. 40

65. Hagedorn, 1999, p. 7

66. Bauer, 1957, p. 832

67. Hagedorn, 1999, p. 7

68. Bauer, 1957, p. 857

69. Walcot, 1978, p. 14

70. ibid., p. 35

71. ibid., p. 35

72. ibid., p. 35

73. ibid., p. 36

74. ibid., p. 36

75. ibid., p. 57

76. ibid., pp. 52-57, 60-61

77. ibid., pp. 56-57

78. ibid., pp. 62-63

79. We will explore the concept of fear of seizure when discussing superstitions surrounding *vaskanía's* social aspects.

80. Walcot, 1978, p. 79

81. ibid., pp. 78-79

82. ibid., p. 65

83. ibid., p. 80

84. Elworthy, Frederick Thomas. *The Evil Eye: An Account of This Ancient and Widespread Superstition*. 1986 ed. New York: Julian Press, 1895., p. 12

85. Siebers, 1983, pp. 84-85

86. Singer, Erwin. *Key Concepts in Psychotherapy*. Second ed. Northvale, NJ: Jason Aronson, Inc., 1965., pp. 249-289

87. Siebers, 1983, p. 85

88. Singer, 1965, pp. 290-312

89. Elliott, John H. "The Evil Eye and the Sermon on the Mount." *Biblical Interpretation* 2, no. 1 (1994): 51-84., pp. 55-56

90. Siebers, 1983, p. 84

91. Elliott, 1994, pp. 56-57

92. Foster, 1972, p. 175; Burke, 1988, p. 217

93. Hardie, Margaret M. "The Evil Eye in Some Greek Villiages of the Upper Haliakmon Valley in West Macedonia." In *The Evil Eye: A Casebook*, edited by Alan Dundes, 107-123. Madison, WI: University of Wisconsen Press, 1923., pp. 112

94. Foster, George. "The Anatomy of Envy: A Study of Symbolic Behavior." *Current Anthropology* 13, no. 2 (1972): 165-186., p. 182

95. ibid., pp. 172-173

96. ibid., p. 183

97. Casalis, Matthieu. "The Dry and the Wet: a Semiological Analysis of Creation and Flood Myths." *Semiotica* 17, no. 1 (1976): 35-67.

98. Casalis first describes the P Creation, which breaks down into nine stages: the Ante-Creation State (Gen 1:2); the Creation of Light (Gen 1:3-5); the Creation of the Sky (Gen 1:6-8); the Creation of the Earth and the Seas (Gen 1:9-10); the Creation of Plants (Gen 1:11-13); the Creation of the Luminaries (Gen 1:14-19); the Creation of Fish and Birds (Gen 1:20-23); the Creation of Earthly Animals (Gen 1:24-25) and the Creation of Man (Gen 1:26-31).

99. We believe this is very important for Christians to remember when dealing with those affiliated with the environmentalist movement. While man can negatively impact the environment in terms of his own comfort levels, there is no ontological possibility of man robbing nature of its ability to produce life. Humans can produce short-term, limited area sterility by creating toxic concentrations, but even our worst environmental disasters have failed to permanently eradicate life from an area. Environmentalists operate with the notion that humans can indeed wipe out all possibility of life. While man can radically impact local or even global climate, the same can be said for any other form of life or even a meteor.

100. The J creation epic consists of six stages : the Ante-creation Stage (Ge 2:4b-6); the Creation of Man (Ge 2:7); the Creation of Plants (Ge 2:8a, 2:9-14); the Settlement of Man (Ge 2:8b, 2:15-17); the Creation of the Animals (Ge 2:18-20) and the Creation of Woman (Ge 2:21-25).

101. Casalis, 1976, pp. 44-47]

102. Trachtenberg, Joshua. *Jewish Magic and Superstition.* 1987 ed. New York: Atheneum, 1939.. Talmud and Midrash are filled with fantastic tales of rabbis zapping people with their eyes. These wild stories show that Evil Eye was thought of strictly as a power of the eyes for evil as part of the "evil inclination" which we might otherwise understand as the "Fall." Rabbis, having lived long lives according to the Law, sometimes were capable of harnessing the power of the Evil Eye for the power of good (or at least self-defense). Obviously, this has enormous ethical consequences, but the rabbis seem wholly non-introspective. They are good, so good that they themselves can use their own personal evil for good. The rabbis' primary biblical defense of this is 2 Kings 2:24 (Elisha curses a group of children mocking him, and bears immediately dash out of the woods and maul the children), which the *Babylonian Talmud* attributes to the Evil Eye of Elisha (Ulmer, p. 84).

103. Ulmer, Rikva. *The Evil Eye in the Bible and Rabbinic Literature.* Hoboken, NJ: KTAV Publishing House, 1994.

104. ibid., pp. 2-4

105. ibid., p. 42

106. Bauer, 1957, p. 690

107. ibid., pp. 690-691

108. Ulmer, 1994, pp. 73-74

109. ibid., pp. 78-79

110. ibid., pp. 73-75

111. ibid., p. 80

112. ibid., pp. 4-5

113. Smith, Louis. "Original is as 'Envy': The Structure of the Biblical Deca-logue." *Dialog* 30, no. 3 (1991): 227-230.

114. Breck, John. "Chiasmus as a Key to Biblical Interpretation." *St. Vladimir's Theological Quarterly* 42, no. 3-4 (1999): 249-267., p. 255

115. Smith, 1991, pp.228-230

116. ibid., p. 230

117. Ulmer, 1994, p. 111

118. ibid., pp. 111-112

119. ibid., pp. 111-113

120. ibid., p. 113

121. ibid., pp. 113-114

122. Tarazi, Paul N. *The Old Testament: An Introduction.* Vol. 1—Historical Traditions. Crestwood, NY: St. Vladimir's Seminary Press, 1991., p.40

123. Brown, Francis, S. R. Driver, and Charles A. Briggs. *The Brown-Driver-Briggs Hebrew and English Lexicon.* 1996 ed. Peabody, MA: Hendrickson Publishers, 1906., p. 888

124. Tarazi, 1991, pp. 34-48

125. ibid., p. 40

126. ibid., pp. 39-40

127. In this case, the Red Sea was a barrier to escape and thus a chaotic water threatening Israel's destruction. The parting of the Red Sea is like the separation of waters leading to creation, but it is also reveals the essential goodness of the water itself: it obeys Yahweh.

128. Siebers, 1983, p. 62

129. The numerous examples of the serpent are too many to catalog here, and we are certain that others have done a far better job exploring all of the possible meanings in the serpent's various appearances in Scripture. Our interest is in the serpent's venomous mouth as a symbol of slander, which is an integral part of the behavior of envy.

130. Pardee, Dennis. "Muerôrat-Puetanîm "venom" in Job 20:14." *Zeitschrift für die Alttestamentliche Wissenschaft* 19, no. 3 (1979): 401-416.

131. ibid., p. 413

132. Waldman, Nahum M. : 199-203.

133. Pardee, 1979, pp. 403-405

134. Joines, Karen R. "The Serpent in Gen 3." *Zeitschrift für die Alttestamentliche Wissenschaft* 87, no. 1 (1975): 1-11.

135. Burke, Joseph. *The Tyranny of Malice: Exploring the Dark Side of Character*. New York: Summit Books, 1988.

136. Tarazi, Paul N. *The New Testament: An Introduction*. Vol. 1—Paul and Mark. Crestwood, NY: St. Vladimir's Seminary Press, 1999., p. 6

137. Johnson, Luke T. "The New Testament's Anti-Jewish Slander and the Conventions of the Ancient Polemic." *Journal of Biblical Literature* 108, no. 3 (1989): 419-441., p. 329

138. Johnson, 1983.

139. ibid., p. 345

140. Tarazi, 1999.

141. Hagedorn, Anselm C., and Jerome H. Neyrey. *"It Was Out of Envy That They Handed Jesus Over" (Mark 15:10): The Anatomy of Envy and the Gospel of Mark* 1999 [cited 03/28/00 2000]. Available from http://www.nd.edu/~jneyrey1/envy.html.

142. ibid., p. 16

143. Obviously, the exact locations and layout of the Temple are subject to debate, especially give the architectural changes between Ezekiel's time and Christ's. It is the association of greed and misuse of animals that grants us the theme, along with the location and the mention of 'seat.'

144. Neyrey, Jerome. *Questions, Chreai, and Challenges to Honor. The Interface of Rhetoric and Culture in Mark's Gospel* 1998 [cited 1 October 2000]. Available from http://www.nd.edu/~jneyrey1/questions.html.

145. Hagedorn, 1999

146. Hagedorn, 1999

147. Hagedorn, 1999

148. Pardee, Dennis. "Muerôrat-Puetanîm "venom" in Job 20:14." *Zeitschrift für die Alttestamentliche Wissenschaft* 19, no. 3 (1979): 401-416.

149. ibid., p. 412

150. Random House, 1987, p. 1272

151. Bauer, 1957, p. 473

152. Ulmer, 1994, p. 78

153. Bauer, 1957, p. 845

154. In the New Testament, only Joseph of Arimathea (Mt 27:57) is considered to be rich and pious, while the typical pious man is Zacchaeus (Lk 19:2-10) who renounced his wealth. In fact, almost all occurrences of 'rich man' (plou, sioj) denote a negative meaning.

155. Elliott, John H. "The Evil Eye and the Sermon on the Mount." *Biblical Interpretation* 2, no. 1 (1994): 51-84., p. 66-67

156. ibid., p. 69

157. Dunbabin, Katherine M. D., and M. W. Dickie. "Invidia Rumpantur Pectora: The Iconography of Phthonos/Invidia In Graeco-Roman Art." *JAC*, no. 26 (1983): 7-37.

158. Luck, Georg. "Witches and Sorcerers in Classical Literature." In *Witchcraft and Magic in Europe: Ancient Greece and Rome*, edited by Bengt Ankarloo and Stuart Clark. Philadelphia: University of Pennsylvania, 1999., p. 155-156

159. Harfouche, Jamal K. "The Evil Eye and Infant Health in Lebanon." In *The Evil Eye: A Casebook*, edited by Alan Dundes, 86-106. Madison, WI: University of Wisconsen Press, 1965., p. 100; Drimeyer, Jack. "Conversation with Father Lawdis." *Hellenic Chronicle*, 4 April 1974, 6.

160. Dunbabin, 1983.

161. Burke, 1988, p. 86

162. Chadwick, Henry. *The Early Church*. 1993 ed. New York: Penguin Books, 1967., pp. 41-43

163. *Dialog with Trypho*, ch. 14

164. *On the Sole Government of God*, ch. 1

165. Russell, Jeffrey B. *Satan: The Early Christian Tradition*. 1994 ed. Ithaca, NY: Cornell University Press, 1981., p. 66

166. ibid., pp. 78-79

167. [St. Athanasius of Alexandria, 321 #118], ch. 29

168. *Against Heresies*, Book 4, 11:3

169. ibid., 40:3; Book 5, 24:4

170. ibid., Book 4, 18:3

171. St. Irenaeus of Lyons. "Against Heresies, Book 5." In *The AGES Digital Library [CD-ROM]*, edited by Alexander Roberts and James Donaldson. Albany, OR: AGES Software, 200., Book 5, 24:4

172. Russell, 1981, pp. 80-81

173. St. Athanasius of Alexandria. "Against the Heathen, Part 2." In *The AGES Digital Library [CD-ROM]*, edited by Archibald Robinson. Albany, OR: AGES Software, 321., ch. 41

174. Louth, Andrew. "Envy as the Chief Sin in Athanasius and Gregory of Nyssa." *Studia Patristica* 15, no. 1 (1980): 458-460.

175. St. Athanasius of Alexandria. "In Defense of His Flight." In *The AGES Digital Library [CD-ROM]*, edited by Archibald Robinson. Albany, OR: AGES Software, 360., ch. 1

176. St. Gregory of Nyssa. *The Life of Moses*. Translated by Malherbe, Abaraham J. Ferguson, Everett. Edited by Richard J. Payne. 1978 ed, *Classics of Western Spirituality*. New York: Paulist Press, 390., para. 256-257

177. St. Gregory of Nyssa. "Oration on Meletius." In *Select Writings and Letters of Gregory, Bishop of Nyssa*, edited by William Moore and Henry A. Wilson. Ann Arbor, MI: Malloy, Inc., 381., pp. 513-514

178. St. Cyprian of Carthage. "On Envy." In *The AGES Digital Library [CD-ROM]*, edited by Alexander Roberts and James Donaldson. Albany, OR: AGES Software, 270.

179. St. Basil the Great. "On Jealousy and Envy." In *St. Basil—Ascetical Works*. New York: Fathers of the Early Church, Inc., 370.

180. Foster, 1965, p. 182; Burke, 1988, pp. 196-197

181. Dickie, 1995, p. 19

182. St. John Chrysostom. "Second Instruction to the Catechumens." In *The AGES Digital Library [CD-ROM]*, edited by Philip Schaff. Albany, OR: AGES Software, 400.

183. Thomsen, Marie-Louise. "The Evil Eye in Mesopotamia." *Journal of Near East Studies*, no. 51 (1992): 19-32., pp.29-30

184. Ulmer, 1994, pp. 148-150

185. Meyer, Marvin. "Greek Texts of Ritual Power from Christian Egypt." In *Ancient Christian Magic*, edited by Marvin Meyer, Richard Smith and Neal Kelsey, 28-57. San Francisco: HarperCollins Publishers, 1994., pp. 49-50

186. Constantinides, Evagoras, ed. *Mikron Evchologion i Agiasmatarion*. Merrillville, IN: Evagoras Constantinides, 1989., p. 194-195

187. St. Tikhon's Monastery, ed. *The Great Book of Needs*. Vol. I—The Holy Mysteries. South Canaan, PA: St. Tikhon's Seminary Press, 1998., p. 4

188. Antiochian Orthodox Christian Archdiocese of North America, ed. *Service Book of the Holy Eastern Orthodox Catholic and Apostolic Church*. 1993 ed. Englewood, NJ: Antiochian Orthodox Christian Archdiocese of North America, 1971., p. 215

189. Bauer, 1957, pp. 136 & 857

190. St. Tikhon's Monastery, ed. *The Great Book of Needs*. Vol. I—The Holy Mysteries. South Canaan, PA: St. Tikhon's Seminary Press, 1998., p. 4

191. We ask the indulgence of those with an eye for detail and minutia to bear with this rapid pass over a exceedingly rich and deep topic. Those interested in exploring any topic presented thus far are strongly urged to consult the bibliography.

192. Thomsen, 1992, pp.26-28

193. Gordon, Richard. "Imagining Greek and Roman Magic." In *Witchcraft and Magic in Europe: Ancient Greece and Rome*, edited by Bengt Ankarloo and Stuart Clark. Philadelphia: University of Pennsylvania, 1999., p. 232

194. Luck, Georg. "Witches and Sorcerers in Classical Literature." In *Witchcraft and Magic in Europe: Ancient Greece and Rome*, edited by Bengt Ankarloo and Stuart Clark. Philadelphia: University of Pennsylvania, 1999., p. 94

195. ibid., pp. 94-96

196. Trachtenberg, Joshua. *Jewish Magic and Superstition*. 1987 ed. New York: Atheneum, 1939.; Schrire, Theodore. *Hebrew Magic Amulets*. 1982 ed. New York: Behrman House, Inc., 1966.

197. Trachtenberg, 1939, pp. 97-99

198. ibid., pp. 54-56, 97

199. ibid., pp. 139-152

200. Elworthy, 1895, p. 241

201. Trachtenberg, 1939, pp. 193-207

202. ibid., p. 7

203. Schrire, Theodore. *Hebrew Magic Amulets*. 1982 ed. New York: Behrman House, Inc., 1966., p. 50

204. Trachtenberg, 1939, p. 37

205. ibid., pp. 57-59

206. ibid., pp. 6-7, 124

207. Hardie, Margaret M. "The Evil Eye in Some Greek Villiages of the Upper Haliakmon Valley in West Macedonia." In *The Evil Eye: A Casebook*, edited by Alan Dundes, 107-123. Madison, WI: University of Wisconsen Press, 1923., p. 111

208. Trachtenberg, 1939, p. 58

209. Harfouche, Jamal K. "The Evil Eye and Infant Health in Lebanon." In *The Evil Eye: A Casebook*, edited by Alan Dundes, 86-106. Madison, WI: University of Wisconsen Press, 1965., p. 95

210. ibid., p. 96

211. Siebers, 1983, pp. 61-63

212. Hardie, 1923, pp. 113-114

213. *Homily 12* on 1 Corinthians 4:6, section 13

214. Tertullian. "On the Veiling of Virgins." In *The AGES Digital Library* *[CD-ROM]*, edited by Alexander Roberts and James Donaldson. Albany, OR: AGES Software, 200., ch. 15 "On Fascination"

215. Hardie, 1923, p. 116

216. Migliore, Sam. *Mal'uocchiu: Ambiguity, Evil Eye, and the Language of Distress*. Toronto: University of Toronto Press, 1997., p. 36-45

217. Hardie, 1923, p. 117

218. Graf, Fritz. *Magic in the Ancient World*. Translated by Philip, Franklin. Edited by G. W. Bowersock. Vol. 10, *Revealing Antiquity*. Cambridge, MA: Harvard University Press, 1997., p. 197

219. Drimeyer, Jack. "Conversation with Father Lawdis." *Hellenic Chronicle*, 4 April 1974, 6.

220. Stanmeyer, Anastasia. "Evil Eye." *The Tampa Tribune*, February 26 1995, 12.

221. Fögen, Marie T. "Balsamon on Magic: From Roman Secular Law to Byzantine Canon Law." In *Byzantine Magic*, edited by Henry Maguire, 99-115. Washington, DC: Dunbarton Oaks, 1995., p. 102

222. Dundes, Alan. "Wet and Dry, the Evil Eye: an Essay in Indo-European and Semitic Worldview." In *The Evil Eye: A Casebook*, edited by Alan Dundes, 257-312. Madison, WI: The University of Wisconsen Press, 1981., pp. 271-273

223. St. John Chrysostom. "Second Instruction to the Catechumens." In *The AGES Digital Library [CD-ROM]*, edited by Philip Schaff. Albany, OR: AGES Software, 400., sect. 5

224. See also St. John's *A Treatise to Prove That No One Can Harm the Man Who Does Not Injure Himself* for a similar diatribe against paranoia of bad luck and worldly circumstances.

225. Holy Trinity Monastery, ed. *The Passion and Miracles of the Great Martyr and Victorious Wonderworker Saint George*. 1957 ed. Jordanville, NY: Holy Trinity Monastery, 1957.

226. Scott Fox, David. *Saint George: The Saint With Three Faces*. Windor Forest, Bershire, UK: The Kensal Press, 1983., p. 12

227. ibid., p. 11

228. ibid., pp. 17-18

229. ibid., p. 13

230. ibid., p. 13

231. Holy Trinity Monastery, ed. *The Passion and Miracles of the Great Martyr and Victorious Wonderworker Saint George*. 1957 ed. Jordanville, NY: Holy Trinity Monastery, 1957., pp. 31-34

232. Scott Fox, 1983, p. 30

233. ibid., p. 24

234. ibid., p. 29

235. ibid., p. 35

236. Nassar, Seraphim, ed. *Divine Prayers and Services of the Catholic Orthodox Church of Christ.* 1993 ed. Englwood, NJ: Antiochian Orthodox Christian Archdiocese of North America, 1938., p. 527

237. Scott Fox, 1983, p. 30

238. ibid., p. 33

239. ibid., p. 34

240. ibid., p. 43

241. ibid., pp. 45-47

242. Luck, Georg. "Witches and Sorcerers in Classical Literature." In *Witchcraft and Magic in Europe: Ancient Greece and Rome,* edited by Bengt Ankarloo and Stuart Clark. Philadelphia: University of Pennsylvania, 1999., pp. 116-117

243. http://www.lib.umich.edu/pap/magic/def1.display.html

244. Nassar, Seraphim, ed. *Divine Prayers and Services of the Catholic Orthodox Church of Christ.* 1993 ed. Englwood, NJ: Antiochian Orthodox Christian Archdiocese of North America, 1938., p. 528

245. Luck, 1999, p. 116; Meyer, Marvin. "Greek Texts of Ritual Power from Christian Egypt." In *Ancient Christian Magic,* edited by Marvin Meyer, Richard Smith and Neal Kelsey, 28-57. San Francisco: HarperCollins Publishers, 1994., pp. 45-46

246. Luck, 1999, p. 117

247. anonymous. *Testament of Solomon* [web page]. Peterson, Joseph H., March 18, 1999 1st—3rd c. AD [cited March 29 2000]. Available from http://www.avesta.org/solomon/testamen.htm., para. 43

248. Scott Fox, 1983, p. 117

249. Meyer, 1994, pp. 47-48

250. Scott Fox, 1983, p. 130

251. Luck, 1999, p. 116

252. Scott Fox, 1983, p. 50

253. al-Ashqar, Umar Sulaiman. *The World of the Jinn and Devils.* Translated by Zarabozo, Jamaal. Boulder, CO: al-Basheer Company for Publications and Translations, 1998., pp. 29-48

254. In the nation of Georgia, the saint bumped out a lunar deity (the Hittite weather god Teshub), and who was tied to the symbol of the horse which he rode. The shoes of the horse resemble the crescent moon, and the dragon has been linked with the moon in terms of its waxing and waning. The darkening of the moon was associated with a dragon trying to swallow it, and so the deity was linked to slaying the monster and freeing the moon once more (Scott Fox, p. 50). Georgians derived their national name from the saint, whom (in some remote areas) was placed above both God the Father and Christ in rank (Scott Fox, 1983, p.120).

0-595-30770-1

13938035R00090

Made in the USA
Lexington, KY
28 February 2012